THE SUMERIANS

By C. LEONARD WOOLLEY

W · W · NORTON & COMPANY

New York · London

TO

MY WIFE

First published in the Norton Library 1965
by arrangement with Oxford University Press

Published simultaneously in Canada by
Penguin Books Canada Ltd,
2801 John Street, Markham, Ontario L3R 1B4.

Books That Live
The Norton imprint on a book means that in the publisher's
estimation it is a book not for a single season but for the years.
W. W. Norton & Company, Inc.

W. W. Norton & Company, Inc., 500 Fifth Avenue, New York, N.Y. 10110
W. W. Norton & Company Ltd., 37 Great Russell Street, London WC1B 3NU

ISBN 0-393-00292-6

PRINTED IN THE UNITED STATES OF AMERICA
1 2 3 4 5 6 7 8 9 0

CONTENTS

I. THE BEGINNINGS

The land of Sumer and Akkad. The peoples of the land. The Semites. The Sumerians. The period of painted pottery. An aboriginal settlement. The growth of the village and the city-state.   *pages* 1–20

II. THE EARLY HISTORY OF SUMER

The King-lists. The Flood. Sumer and Akkad. The dynasties of Kish and Erech. The palace of Kish. The Royal Graves at Ur. The temple at al-'Ubaid. The First Dynasty of Ur. Early Sumerian art. The extension of early Sumerian culture. The Sumerian Army.

pages 21–61

III. THE PERIOD OF CIVIL WARS

The rise of Lagash: Eannatum; Uru-kagina. The conquests of Lugal-zaggisi. Sargon of Akkad; the growing power of the Semites. The Dynasty of Agade. The Guti invasion. Sumer under the Guti: Urbau; Gudea.

pages 62–89

IV. SUMERIAN SOCIETY

Civil law. The Code of Hammurabi and the older codes. Castes. Slavery. Marriage and divorce. Children and adoption. Religious prostitution. Schools and education. Agriculture. Foreign trade and credit. Religious beliefs. The future life. The legends of the Flood and the Creation. A religion of Fear. Sacrifices and charms. Soothsaying; omens and astrology. Religion and the State.

pages 90–129

Contents

V. THE THIRD DYNASTY OF UR

Ur-Nammu; public works and monuments. Dungi; the organization of the Empire. The Capital of the Empire in the great days;—the Ziggurat;—the temple of Nannar;—E-nun-makh;—Dublal-makh;—temple factories;—Gigpar-ku;—private houses;—graves;—sculpture. Reign of Bur-Sin. Ibi-Sin. The collapse of the Third Dynasty.

pages 130–169

VI. ISIN AND LARSA

The rise of Isin. The survival of Sumerian prestige. Larsa under the Elamite Dynasty. The rise of Babylon. Literary activity under the Larsa kings. Hammurabi. The end of the Sumerians. *pages* 170–181

VII. THE CLAIM OF SUMER *pages* 181–193

INDEX

I

THE BEGINNINGS

BY the second millennium before Christ the formula used by Mesopotamian kings to show that their power extended over the whole Land of the Two Rivers was 'King of Sumer and Akkad'. The great alluvial plain from the site of the modern city of Baghdad, where the Tigris and the Euphrates approach most closely to each other, down to a point a little below Kurna, where was then the head of the Gulf, was divided into two parts; the boundary between these was ill-defined, shifting this way and that with the vicissitudes of conquest and with the rise and fall of rival elements in the population, but in the main the two countries stood in sharp opposition to one another, distinguished by the race and language of those who lived in them: Akkad, in the north, was predominantly Semitic; Sumer, in the south, was more mixed, but the Semitic element here was swamped by the Sumerians who had imposed on it their language and their civilization and had the land called after their own name.

Lower Mesopotamia, which includes both Sumer and Akkad, is a delta redeemed from the Persian Gulf whose waters once reached nearly as far north as Hit, and it is a delta of very recent formation. The upper Euphrates valley and the high plateau of the Syrian desert had been inhabited by man long before the gulf waters had receded: there the monuments of the palaeolithic age abound, and the later stone age has left its traces in the valleys of the Euphrates, the Khabur and the Sajur, but in Mesopotamia itself nothing of the kind is found: in the earliest human settlements flint instruments indeed are common, but they are associated with metal or betray the influence of metal-working, and we can only conclude that it was comparatively late in human history, when man had already advanced into the calcholithic age, that the lower valley became fit for his occupation.

Just by the modern town of Muhammerah in Persia, where in old days stretched the waters of the greater gulf, the river Karun empties into the Shatt al-Arab. Almost opposite to it is the Wadi al-Batin, now dry but once a great river running up from the heart of Arabia. The Karun brings down from the Persian hills as much silt as do the waters of the Tigris and the Euphrates combined, and the old al-Batin stream, though more sluggish, must have been almost as rich in silt; in the course of time the mud discharged by them into the gulf massed below their mouths in banks which gradually advancing across the gulf joined up and made a bar from shore to shore. The bar neutralized the scouring action of the gulf tide and enabled the Tigris and the Euphrates to deposit at their mouths the silt which had hitherto been swept out to sea, and at the same time the silt of the southern rivers began to fill in what had now become a great lagoon, while the waters of all of them joined in turning it gradually from salt to brackish and from brackish to fresh. The mud of the two northern streams that did not go to swell the delta now forming at their mouths was dropped, now that the current was checked by the bar, over the whole of the old gulf area and helped to raise the level of its bed; thus, while dry land was formed first and most quickly in the north and in the south, the lagoon between grew more and more shallow, islands appeared, and at last where all had been a waste of water there stretched a vast delta of clay and sand and mud, diversified by marshes and reed-beds, through which wound rivers so flush with their banks that they were for ever changing their courses: it was a delta periodically flooded, and in the summer scorched by a pitiless sun, but its soil, light and stoneless, was as rich as could be found anywhere on earth, and scarcely needed man's labour to produce man's food. The description in Genesis of the creation of the earth as man's home agrees admirably with the process of the formation of the Mesopotamian delta: 'Let the waters under the heaven be gathered together unto one place, and let the dry land appear: and it was so. . . . And the earth brought forth grass, and herb yielding seed after his kind, and the tree yielding fruit, whose seed was in itself, after his kind: and God saw that it was good.'

The manner in which the land formed is important as serving to explain the differences in the population that occupied it. A country so rich potentially invited settlers, and these were forthcoming, but they must have come in gradually as the process of transformation took place, and they did not come from the same regions, but from all the shores of the ancient gulf.

The northern part of the Syrian desert and the upper Euphrates valley were inhabited by a people of Semitic speech known, when they first appear in history, as the Martu or, later, as the Amurru. It was natural that as the delta formed in the north at the mouth of the Euphrates the new land should be colonized by these neighbouring folk following the retreating waters and cultivating the freshly-dried alluvium: they occupied Sippar and Opis, on either side of the neck of land where the two rivers come closest together, and thereby secured possession of the northern triangle which was to be the land of Akkad. To the north and east of them, in the Zagros hills and across the plain to the Tigris, there lived a people of very different stock, fair-haired and speaking a 'Caucasian' tongue, a hill-people akin to the Guti who were to play no small part in Sumerian history; they seem to have moved down into the Tigris valley, but their advance south was blocked by the Martu occupation of the land neck, so that they failed to gain a footing in the new delta and remained in what was afterwards Assyria, the neighbour land to Akkad.

Scattered over the central Arabian plateau were the ancestors of the modern Beduin and these nomads also took advantage of the rich opportunities offered by the drying up of the lower delta to change their mode of life, individual families or clans drifting down from the desert uplands into the marshes wherever an island site made agriculture possible. Thus into Sumer there came a Semitic element which was quite distinct from the Semitic population of Akkad; except for a similarity of language (and even here the dialects must have been very different) they had little in common with them and certainly had not attained anything like the same degree of civilization. The colonists of Akkad, coming from a comparatively civilized home-land with which they needed not to lose touch, were better organized and capable of common action, so that city life would have been possible from the beginning: the southern Semites were strangers to town life, owing to the nature of the marshy country their occupation of it would tend to be more sporadic, and both character and circumstances would prevent such social unity. as would enable them to hold their own against neighbours better equipped.

The last of the incomers were the Sumerians. These were a dark-haired people—'black-heads', the texts call them—speaking an agglutinative language somewhat resembling ancient Turkish (Turanian) in its formation though not in its etymology; judging by their physical type they were of the Indo-European stock, in appearance not unlike the modern Arab,[1] and were certainly

[1] 'The Mesopotamian peoples, both past and present, represent a transition between Iranian and Semitic types, but they have retained more of the Iranian than of the Semite. . . . As to the racial nature of the al-'Ubaid people there cannot be any doubt; if they were living to-day we should call them Arabs. . . . There is no trace . . . of any round-headed element of the Hittite type nor of a Mongolian type. . . . The southern Mesopotamians at the beginning of the fourth millennium B.C. had big, long and narrow heads; their affinities were with the peoples of the Caucasian or European type, and we may regard south-western Asia as their cradleland until evidence leading to a different con-

well developed intellectually. What their original home was we do not know. The fact that Sumerian gods are constantly represented as standing upon mountains would imply that the people came from a hill country; that their earliest building style is based on a tradition of timber construction is an argument to the same conclusion, for such could only originate in the heavily-timbered uplands; the description given in Genesis, 'and the people journeyed from the east and came into the plain of Shinar and dwelt there', refers to the Sumerians and must incorporate some Sumerian legend as to their own movements; but the obvious conclusion that they descended from the Elamite mountains which border the delta valley on the east does not meet the case, for though there are common elements in the early cultures of Mesopotamia and Elam it does not seem possible to derive the Sumerian from the latter, nor does the physical type show identity of race: Sumerian legends which

clusion comes to light. They were akin to the predynastic people of Egypt described by Dr. Foquet, but differed from all other predynastic and dynastic Egyptians. The Neolithic people of English long barrows were also related to them—perhaps distantly; the Sumerian type made its appearance in Europe in Palaeolithic times, for one of the earliest of Aurignacian skulls—that found at Combe Capelle in the Dordogne, France, is near akin to the ancient Arab type.' Sir Arthur Keith in *Al-'Ubaid*, pp. 216, 240.

explain the beginnings of civilization in Mesopotamia seem to imply an influx of people from
the sea, which people can scarcely be other than
the Sumerians themselves, and the fact that the
historic Sumerians are at home in the south country
and that Eridu, the city reputed by them to be
the oldest in the land, is the southernmost of all,
supports that implication. Sir Arthur Keith states:[1]
'One can still trace the ancient Sumerian face
eastwards among the inhabitants of Afghanistan
and Baluchistan, until the valley of the Indus is
reached—some 1,500 miles distant from Mesopotamia.' Recent excavation in the Indus valley has
brought to light extensive remains of a very early
civilization, remarkably developed, which has a
good deal in common with that of Sumer; particularly striking are rectangular stamp seals found
in the two countries which are identical in form, in
the subjects and style of their engraving, and in the
inscriptions which they bear, while there are simi-
larities hardly less marked in terra-cotta figures,
in the methods of building construction and in
ground-plans. To say that these resemblances
prove identity of race or even political unity would
be to exaggerate the weight of the evidence; to
account for them by mere trade connexion would
be, in my opinion, to underrate it no less rashly: it

[1] *Al-'Ubaid*, p. 216.

is safest, for the time being, to regard the two civilizations as offshoots from a common source which presumably lies somewhere between the Indus and the Euphrates valleys, though whether the centre from which this culture radiates so far afield is to be sought in the hills of Baluchistan, or where, we have no means of knowing as yet.

There is another factor which further complicates the question. The oldest levels yet tapped in southern Mesopotamia produce a very fine painted pottery which disappears entirely before the beginning of the historic period as we know it, i.e. before the earliest of the graves at Ur which must date to about 3500 B.C. The pots are hand-made or, more rarely, turned on the slow-moving wheel, the *tournette*; the walls, of greenish grey, buff or red ware, are sometimes extremely thin, and are ornamented with a decoration built up from simple geometric motives executed in a brown or black semi-lustrous paint. Between this pottery and that found in the lowest levels at Susa, at Musyan in Elam and at Bushire on the Persian Gulf, there are points of resemblance which undoubtedly connote a certain relation and have by some writers been taken to prove a close parentage; actually there are also points of difference which make such close parentage impossible. The Mesopotamian ware is older in time than the Elamite and belongs to a considerably earlier stage of development, so that it cannot be derived from the Elamite; consequently it supplies no evidence for the Sumerians being descended from Elam. Further, we cannot even be sure that the Mesopotamian pottery is Sumerian at all: Campbell Thompson, who first drew attention to it at Eridu, considered it to be pre-Sumerian, and this may very well be true. At a place called Jemdet Nasr near Kish painted pottery distinct from that of the southern Sumerian sites, later in date and more nearly resembling the Musyan wares, has been found associated with very early clay tablets inscribed with a semi-pictographic script, but this discovery only proves that at Kish painted pottery survived into the period of Sumerian culture, it does not establish its authorship. As painted wares of very early date also having points of resemblance to and of difference from those of southern Mesopotamia occur further to the north and as far west as Carchemish, where a Sumerian population cannot have existed at that time, the case for the Sumerian origin of the Mesopotamian pottery is weakened and that for the Elamite origin of the Sumerian people disappears. Who then can have been responsible for this distinctive and almost sole surviving product of the earliest occupation of the lower river valley? It is highly improbable that the finely made and

I. STELA OF UR-NAMMU

Fragment, partly restored. The King pours libations to Nannar and Nin-Gal, and receives
the order to build the Ziggurat of Ur; *below*, the King comes with the tools of a workman to
lay the foundations of the building

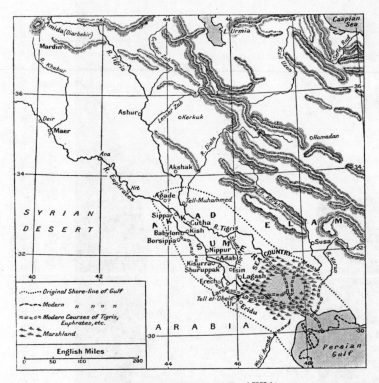

2. MAP OF SUMER AND AKKAD

*From Harmsworth's "Universal History of the World,"
by permission of the Amalgamated Press, Ltd.*

3. THE HEAD-DRESS OF QUEEN SHUB-AD

The face, modelled by Katharine Woolley over a female skull of
the period, reproduces as exactly as possible the physical type of
the original. The dimensions of the wig were given by the gold
ribbons of the head-dress; the arrangement of the hair is based on
(later) terra-cottas. All the details of the head-dress, wreaths, &c.,
are in their original order

4. PRE-SUMERIAN PAINTED POTTERY FROM AL-ʿUBAID

After a drawing by F. G. Newton

From Smith, "Early History of Assyria," by permission of Messrs. Chatto and Windus

Iraq Museum, Baghdad. Upper photograph by Mansell

5. FRIEZE FROM THE TEMPLE AT AL-ʿUBAID

Mosaic in limestone and shale. A cattle byre with temple servants milking the cows and straining and storing the milk. 3100 B.C.

6. THE HARP OF QUEEN SHUB-AD

(Restored)

7. SHELL INLAY FROM THE PALACE AT KISH

The art is Sumerian, but the figures may represent Akkadians

Iraq Museum, Baghdad. From Langdon, "Excavations at Kish," Vol. I
(Paul Geuthner), by permission

8. BRICK ARCHED DOORWAY AND VAULT OF THE FOURTH MILLENNIUM B.C.

The tomb chamber in the King's grave at Ur

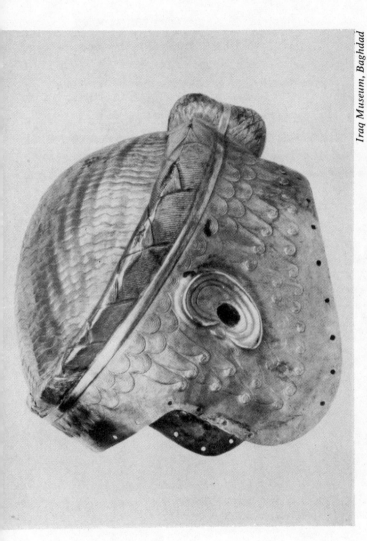

Iraq Museum, Baghdad

9. THE GOLDEN HELMET OF MES-KALAM-DUG

The most striking example of Sumerian goldsmiths' work, dating from before
the First Dynasty of Ur

10. THE TEMPLE AT AL-ʿUBAID

Restoration of the façade, showing the order of the friezes and the porch with columns
of mosaic and copper, copper lions, and relief

11. SHELL PLAQUES ENGRAVED WITH
MYTHOLOGICAL SCENES

From a harp (?) decorated with a bull's head in gold
and lapis lazuli found in the King's grave at Ur

University Museum, Philadelphia

12. GOLD VASES FROM THE ROYAL GRAVES AT UR

13. SILVER COW'S HEAD FROM THE GRAVE OF
QUEEN SHUB-AD AT UR

beautifully decorated pottery of Eridu, Ur and al-'Ubaid was the handiwork of Semitic colonists from central Arabia; desert nomads are by reason of their manner of life unready potters, and what we know of later Arabian pottery would not lead us to suspect so artistic a beginning. Perhaps the real clue is given by the parallels noted in the far north. At Ur we have found a crude painted clay figurine of a man, contemporary with the decorated vases, who wears a long thin pointed beard quite unlike anything represented on the oldest Sumerian works of art but curiously like certain figures on mother-of-pearl inlays from Kish, which is an Akkadian, not a Sumerian centre; the painted pottery may be of Akkadian origin. In that case its occurrence at Eridu and Ur may mean that the Martu, who, for all that their speech in historic times was Semitic, must have been of Asia Minor stock, pushed down further south than has been supposed and controlled the country and its scattered population of Arabian colonists as far as the shores of the Persian Gulf, that, in other words, an Akkadian Mesopotamia preceded the incoming of the Sumerians and that the division of the land as we know it later resulted from the driving back of its earliest rulers by invaders from the sea.

Of the three elements then the Sumerians were probably the last to enter the south country. They

came from a distance and were not likely to be
tempted to migrate so far until the land was sufficiently formed to offer reasonable facilities for
agriculture and for commerce, whereas the Semitic
nomads were on the spot and would naturally
have moved down on to the fertile soil as it appeared. 'Mankind when created did not know of
bread for eating or garments for wearing. The
people walked with limbs on the ground, they ate
herbs with their mouths like sheep, they drank
ditch-water', says a Sumerian hymn, and the description, which scarcely fits the Sumerians themselves as the apostles of civilization, would be apt
enough for the despised dwellers in the swamps
whom the new-comers found on their arrival and
enslaved to their service.

The account given by the Babylonians of how
civilization was introduced (cf. p. 189) implies
that there were already people in the land and that
their manner of life must have been very much that
described in the hymn.

A glimpse of these marsh-dwellers is afforded by
the excavation at al-'Ubaid near Ur of a primitive
settlement of the painted pottery age. Upon a low
mound rising above the level of the flooded land
there was planted a village made up of little huts
whose walls were of reed matting stretched between wooden uprights and waterproofed with

pitch or with a thick mud plaster; their roofs were flat, of mud spread over mats supported by cross beams, or else arched like those of many modern huts in the district, in which bundles of tall reeds tied together serve instead of the wooden uprights and the tops of each facing pair are bent inwards and lashed together so as to form a series of arches, then horizontal ribs of reed are tied to these and reed mats laid over the whole. The huts had wooden doors whose hinge-poles revolved on sockets of imported stone, and the hearths were either holes in the beaten mud floor or were built up with bricks of unbaked mud. Cows, sheep, goats and pigs were kept; barley was grown, and the people ground it in rough querns or pounded it in mortars to make a kind of porridge, and fish was a staple article of food. Copper was known, but was still a luxury; for most purposes stone was used, and small knives, saws, the cutters of the threshing-machines, arrow-heads and so on were chipped out from flint or chert picked up in the high desert or from translucent obsidian, like bottle-glass, imported from the far-off Caucasus. Indeed metal was so rare that the sickles for cutting the barley were made of baked clay, and because these so quickly broke or grew blunt and were thrown away we find hundreds of them strewing the ancient sites. Bone was used for awls and netting-needles. Besides the painted pots, there were coarser clay wares, sometimes with incised decoration, and food-bowls of limestone for those that could afford such. The villagers went on the marshes in narrow canoe-shaped boats with high curled prows made of reeds tied together. They wore garments of sheepskin or of homespun cloth, and judging from the painted marks on a clay figurine they may have tattooed their bodies: their ears were pierced to take studs of bone, bitumen or baked clay, and the women wore heavy necklaces of beads roughly chipped from crystal, carnelian and shell and dressed their hair in a 'bun' at the back of the head; the men seem to have had long pointed beards. They buried their dead in the earth lying on one side with the knees bent, and as they placed with them offerings of food, personal ornaments, tools, &c., we may suppose that they had some kind of belief in the continuation of life after death.

It is impossible to assign even an approximate date to the village settlement of al-'Ubaid; only the presence of the painted pottery shows that it must have flourished very long before the semi-historic age which is illustrated by the excavations of Kish and Ur and can be brought into relation with the written records of the Sumerians. But it does throw some light upon the conditions of life in the delta when human occupation was still in its early phases, conditions which otherwise we can only deduce from the natural course of events and from what we find to have evolved in later times.

One must picture the opening stage as one in which isolated settlers ventured into the drying marsh, put up their reed huts on natural islands or raised them on just such platforms of reeds and mud as are described in the Babylonian Epic of Creation, according to which Marduk kneaded clay and spread it over a mat made of rushes which he laid on the face of the waters, and began to cultivate their little patch of ground, trenching it for drainage or digging channels for its more regular irrigation. On the wider stretches of land, and especially along the river's banks where the soil was richest, villages would grow up, and with their growth would come in corporate effort leading to the construction of more important canals and to something like the scientific control of the river. With the advent of the Sumerians, who seem to have been pre-eminently town-dwellers, a further development took place.

The conditions of the earliest settlement and the physical character of the country at the time made inevitable the segregation of each little colony, intent upon putting as much land as possible under cultivation and cut off from any neighbours by barren reaches of marsh. As the gradual drying of the land did away with the marsh barriers, the separate communities were brought not only into touch but into competition with each other; all were afflicted with land-hunger, the soil naturally fertile was limited and the reclamation of the No-man's Land would lead to quarrels between neighbours; canals dug to water a wider area might pass by or across the territory of another village which could tap its waters for the benefit of their own lands; cattle-lifting was easier and quicker than cattle-breeding; disputes over land, water, and flocks must have been common and forced men to band themselves together for protection against enemies around them. Experience had taught that buildings made of mud or sun-dried brick had to be raised above water-level, on an artificial platform, if needs be, and that an earthen rampart was the best thing to keep out the recurrent floods; common sense remarked that a rampart more sheerly built would keep out an enemy also, and so the village developed into a walled town. Such a town became the centre and the place of refuge for the surrounding district where the inhabitants of scattered farms and hamlets were too weak to protect themselves; Sumerian genius introduced or evolved a system of government; the building in the town of a temple to that god of the pantheon who was most in favour with the settlers and the recognition of him as the town's peculiar patron gave religious sanction to the principle of local autonomy; the *patesi* or chief priest of the temple, as the god's direct representative on earth, naturally, in a theocratic state, assumed the position and powers of civil governor: from a very early date Mesopotamia became a land of small city-states.

The result, though inevitable, was not really a logical one. Throughout the whole country the Sumerians, as we shall see, were predominant, and there was to that extent at least a homogeneous population. They had imposed everywhere the same material civilization; the Sumerian language, used exclusively in the south, had its vogue in the north also, and law and custom were uniform; even the religion was the same, in spite of the emphasis on individual deities which served to differentiate the city-states. The unification of the country was obviously the next step forward, and a very necessary one if the rich agricultural valley was to be safeguarded against attack from without; two things hindered it, the incessant quarrels over land and water, and the local patriotism which grew up in the population of the several states.

The clash of these two motives, for centralization and disruption, explain in a measure the subsequent history of Sumer. The ordinary citizen, husbandman or merchant, demanded primarily from his government peace and respect for the rights of property, together with such aggrandizement as circumstances might afford. Since most troubles had their roots in quarrels over land and were due to the action or the existence of independent neighbouring states, the surest way to stop them was to suppress that independence and establish a single government. This gave a ready handle to the ambition of a governor, and just because there was so much in common between the populations of the various cities the vanquished might acquiesce without too much difficulty in the domination of a kindred neighbour; the change of government need not involve oppression and it did secure peace. But such domination rested entirely on force, and power was unstable; let the suzerain once be weakened by intrigue at home or by a blow dealt by some foreign enemy and there was no traditional loyalty to prop up his authority; every city had as good a claim to rule as any other, and its governors, if they entertained the ambition to empire, could count on the old sectarian spirit to back their rebellion. Civil war was the rule rather than the exception.

The above is an attempt to reconstruct the history of the beginnings of Sumer from very intangible evidence. There is no written record of this early period and very few archaeological data have as yet come to light; geography and ethnology afford suggestions rather than facts, and for the rest we must deduce from the conditions of a later age the chain of events that led up to them: rightly or wrongly imagined, our sketch has brought us to the time when history begins, and before going further we must turn aside to see what are the sources on which that history rests.

THE KING-LISTS (Ch. II)

A. THE KINGS BEFORE THE FLOOD. (Larsa list No. 1.)

Name	City	Length of Reign
A-lu-lim	NUN[KI]	8 sars=28,800 years
A-la(l)-gar	NUN[KI]	10 sars=36,000 years
En-me-en-lu-an-na	Bad-tabira	12 sars=43,200 years
En-me-en-gal-an-na	Bad-tabira	8 sars=28,800 years
Dumuzi 'the shepherd'	Bad-tabira	10 sars=36,000 years
En-Sib-zi-an-na	Larak	8 sars=28,800 years
En-me-en-dur-an-na	Sippar	5 sars, 5 ners=21,000 years
(?) du-du	Suruppak	5 sars, 1 ner=18,600 years

(Total) 8 kings, 5 cities, 241,200 years

'The Flood came. After the Flood came, kingship was sent down from on high.'

B. THE KINGS AFTER THE FLOOD. (Larsa list.)

The First Dynasty of KISH

1. GA-UR	1,200 years		10. A-tab	600 years
2. GUL-la-[d]NIDABA-an-na	960 years		11. A-tab-ba	840 years
3. (?)			12. Ar-pi-um	720 years
4. (?)			13. Etana the shepherd	1,500 years
5. Ba-....			14. Ba-li-ih	400 years
6. (?)			15. En-me-nun-na	660 years
7. Ga-li-bu-um	360 years		16. Me-lam-Kish	900 years
8. Ka-lu-mu-mu	840 years		17. Bar-rak-nun-na	1,200 years
9. Ka-ga-gi-ib	900 years		18. Mes-za- (?)	140 years

19. Ti-iz-gar	306 years	22. En-me-en-bara-gi-si	900 years
20. Il-ku-u	900 years	23. Ag-ga	625 years
21. Il-ta-sa-du-um	1,200 years		

(Total) 23 kings, 24,510 years 3 months 3½ days.

The First Dynasty of ERECH

1. Mes-ki-ag-ga-se-ir (son of the Sun-god)	325 years	6. Ur-dNungal	30 years
2. En-me-kar	420 years	7. Utul-kalamma	15 years
3. (The god) Lugalbanda, the shepherd	1,200 years	8. Labasher	9 years
		9. Ennunadanna	8 years
4. (The god) Dumuzi, the fisher-man	100 years	10. . . . -he-de	36 years
		11. Me-lam-an-na	6 years
5. Gilgamish lord of Kullab	126 years	12. Lugal-ki-aga	36 years

(Total) 12 kings, 2,310 years.

The First Dynasty of UR
(About 3100–2930 B.C.)

1. Mes-an-ni-pad-da	80 years	3. Elulu	25 years
(1A. A-an-ni-pad-da)		4. Balulu	36 years
2. Mes-ki-ag-dNannar	36 years		

(Total) 4 kings (should be five), 177 years.

The Dynasty of AWAN

(Total) 3 kings, 356 years.

The Second Dynasty of KISH

1. (?)		5. KU-E	300 years
2. Da-da-sig	201 years	6. ...: nun-na	180 years
3. Ma-ma-gal-la	(?)	7. I-bi-ni-...	290 years
4. Ka-al-bu- ...	360 years	8. Lugal-mu	360 years
	195 years		

(Total) 8 kings, 3,195 years.

The Dynasty of HAMASI

Hadanish   360 years

(Total) 1 king, 360 years.

The Second Dynasty of ERECH

1. En-uk-du-an-na   60 years

(Total) Kingship lasted 120 years. They ruled 480 years.

The Second Dynasty of UR

4 kings, 108 years, according to the Nippur list.

The Dynasty of ADAB

1. Lugal-an-ni-mu-un-du   90 years

(Total) 1 king, 90 years.

The Dynasty of MARI

1. An-pu	30 years	4. ... -lugal-gal	20 years
2. ... -zi	(?)	5. ... -bi-im	30 years
3. ... -lugal	30 years	6.	9 years

(Total) 6 kings, 136 years.

The Third Dynasty of KISH

KU-dBau, a woman wine-seller   100 years

NOTE.—The dynasties given above must in many cases have been more or less contemporary, but nothing is known about them; from this time onward the amount of overlap can be checked and the dynasties are therefore printed in parallel columns.

The Dynasty of AKSHAK

Unzi	30 years
Undalulu	6 years
Urur	6 years
Puzur-sahan	20 years
Ishu-il	24 years
Gimil-Sin	7 years

The Dynasty of AGADE
(About 2630–2470 B.C.)

Sargon	55 years
Rimush	9 years
Manishtusu	15 years
Naram-Sin	55 years
Shargalisharri	24 years
'Who was king, who was not king?'	

The Fourth Dynasty of KISH
(About 2650 B.C.)

Puzur-Sin	25 years
Ur-Ilbaba	6 (?) years
Zimudar	30 years
Usi-watar	6 years
Ishtar-muti	11 years
Ishme-Shamash	11 years
Nannia'	3 years

The Dynasty of GUTIUM
(About 2470 B.C.)

Imta	3 years
Inkishu	6 years

Patesis of LAGASH

Ur-Nina (about 2900 B.C.)
Akurgal
Eannatum I
Enannatum I
Entemena
Enannatum II
Enetarzi
Enlitarri
Lugal-anda
Urukagina (about 2630 B.C.)

The Third Dynasty of ERECH
(About 2630 B.C.)

Lugal-zaggisi   25 years

The Fourth Dynasty of ERECH
(About 2470 B.C.)

Ur-nigin	7 years
Ur-gigir	6 years

Patesis of LAGASH

Ur-Bau
Nam-makhni
Ur-gar
Dar-azag
Lu-Bau
Lu-Gula
Gudea
Ur-Ningirsu
Ur-lama
Kudda — 6 years
Puzur-ili — 5 years
Ur-Babbar — 6 years

Nikillagab	6 years
Shulme	6 years
Elulumesh	6 years
Inimabakesh	5 years
Igeshaush	6 years
Iarlagab	15 years
Ibate	3 years
Iarlagash	3 years
Kurum	1 year
......	3 years
......	2 years
Irarum	2 years
Ibranum	1 year
Hablum	2 years
Puzur-Sin	7 years
Iarlaganda	7 years
......	7 years
Tirigan	40 days

The Third Dynasty of UR
(About 2278–2170 B.C.)

Ur-Nammu	18 years
Dungi	47 years
Bur-Sin	9 years
Gimil-Sin	9 years
Ibi-Sin	25 years

The Dynasty of ISIN
(About 2170–1950 B.C.)

Ishbi-Irra	32 years
Gimil-ilishu	10 years
Idin-Dagan	21 years
Ishme-Dagan	20 years
Libit-Ishtar	11 years

The Fifth Dynasty of ERECH
(About 2280 B.C.)

Utu-khegal	7 years

The Dynasty of LARSA
(About 2170–1910 B.C.)

Naplanum	
Emisu	28 years
Samum	35 years
Zabaia	9 years

The First Dynasty of BABYLON
(About 2040 B.C.)

Sumu-abu	14 years
Sumu-la-ilu	36 years
Zabum	14 years
Apil-Sin	18 years
Sin-muballit	29 years
Hammurabi (1940 B.C.)	43 years

The Dynasty of ISIN
(continued)

Ur-Enurta	28 years
Bur-Sin	21 years
Libit-Enlil	5 years
Irra-mitti	8 years
Enlil-bani	24 years
Zambia	3 years
Iter-pisha	5 years
Ur-dukuga	4 years
Sin-magir	11 years
Damiq-ilishu	

The Dynasty of LARSA
(continued)

Gungunum	27 years
Abi-sare	11 years
Sumu-ilu	29 years
Nur-Adad	16 years
Sin-idinnam	6 years
Sin-eribam	2 years
Sin-iqisham	5 years
Silli-Adad	1 year
The Elamite Kings of LARSA	
Warad-Sin, son of Kudur-Mabug	12 years
Rim-Sin	61 years

N.B.—The dates prior to the Third Dynasty of Ur are given in round figures and are approximate only; in the early period there is a margin of error of about one hundred years.

II

THE EARLY HISTORY OF SUMER

THE main written sources for the history of the early periods are the lists of kings, certain legends, references to events in omen-texts, and, later, royal inscriptions and the year-names of the kings. The results of excavations at Kish, Fara, Ur, al-'Ubaid, Tello, Warka, Nippur, and Asshur, to mention the most important sites, have done much to illustrate the written records and to add to the scanty information which they contain.

About 2000 B.C., after the fall of the Third Dynasty of Ur, Sumerian scribes took it in hand to record the glories of the great days that had passed away. They must have had at their disposal a mass of documentary evidence, and from this they compiled on the one hand the political history and on the other the religious traditions of the land. Their histories have perished, or survive only in excerpts embodied in Babylonian chronicles of much later date, but there do remain contemporary copies of the schematic lists of kings which they drew up as the framework of their narrative and, for the earliest part, a version made by the priest Berossus in the Greek period.

The list gives the names of kings arranged in

their dynasties, the number of years of the reign of each, and the total for the dynasty; it starts with ten kings who reigned before the Flood and details nineteen dynasties which bridged the long period between the Flood and the close of the Third Dynasty of Ur. Unfortunately the list, as an historical instrument, is of unequal and uncertain value. When they are dealing with times not too far removed from their own and could consult contemporary monuments or trustworthy records the scribes' statements can be accepted so far as they go, but even here may be misunderstood. The dynasties, as written down, would appear to be consecutive, so that by simple dead reckoning we might obtain the date of any king, but actually some of them are in whole or in part contemporary; one starts with the natural supposition that the kings are suzerains of the whole country, but from the fact of their overlapping it is clear that some at least could not substantiate the claim, and it is hard to understand why they are included, especially when no mention is made of kings whom we know to have exercised a rule limited indeed but none the less important. For the purposes of chronology therefore the figures given by the scribes have to be checked and modified by such outside information as is available, and this on so generous a scale that the date of about 4600 B.C. which the sum of their figures would ascribe to the First Dynasty of Ur must be brought down to about 3100 B.C.

The ten antediluvian kings are credited with reigns which added together make the modest total of 241,200 years according to one list (which gives only eight names) or, according to the other, 456,000. The figures are in multiples of *sars* or cycles of 360 years each; behind these grotesque sums there may be some confusion between different systems of notation, but even so another schematizing influence has been at work and it is not difficult to see that numbers have been modified or invented to harmonize with some theory of astronomy. Even in the list of the first two dynasties that ruled after the Flood and before the First Dynasty of Ur, though the scheme on which the figures are based is not the same (reigns are not reckoned by *sars*), an exaggeration hardly less gross deprives them of any dating value: of the kings of Kish one is credited with 1,500 years and three with 1,200 each, and the twenty-three kings between them account for 24,510 years 3 months 3½ days; the twelve kings of Erech rule for 2,310 years.

Another point on which criticism has been directed is that amongst the names of the kings occur some which reappear later as those of gods

or heroes of mythological legends. The antediluvian Dumuzi is Tammuz or Adonis, the vegeta-
tion-god who dies in winter and is revived each
spring, and he figures again in the dynasty of
Erech; Gilgamesh of Erech is the hero of the great
legend of which the Flood epic forms a part;
Lugalbanda 'the shepherd' is a god, Mes-ki-ag-ga-
se-ir is a son of the Sun-god, and Etana 'the shepherd' is a hero who flew to heaven on the back of
an eagle; it is only when we come to the last seven
names of the dynasty of Erech that the kings lose
their divinity and the years of their reigns become
consistent with the span of mortal life.

Are the king-lists then to be dismissed as mere
fables? Until recently none of the names given
was substantiated by contemporary documents
until the Third Dynasty of Kish, the eighth in
order after the Flood: now the discovery of monuments of the First Dynasty of Ur, the third after
the Flood, confirms its historical character, and
certainly encourages one to suspect a substratum
of fact under the fantastic dates and divine names
of the prehistoric period. The names indeed need
cause little difficulty. At a later time Sumerian
kings were deified after death and even in their lifetime; there is no reason to suppose that the practice
was an innovation, on the contrary the human sacrifices which accompany the burials of the earliest

rulers whereas the graves of commoners do not at any period show traces even of a survival of such honours may well be interpreted as evidence that the king was distinguished from his subjects by the attribute of divinity; and round the memory of a deified king legend was sure to gather. That the Babylonians themselves regarded Gilgamesh as a human ruler and a builder of walls still extant in their day is not a proof, but it is a pointer; we need not try to make history out of the legends, but we ought to assume that beneath much that is artificial or incredible there lurks something of fact.

The mere fact that the scribes recorded antediluvian kings and mention cities which existed before the Flood must signify that the Sumerian occupation of the country dated from before that great disaster. The king-lists only mention the Flood, the description of it is preserved in the well-known Deluge Epic and, of course, in that variant which is the Flood story of Genesis. However much tradition may have magnified and coloured the account, it would be absurd to deny the ultimately historical character of a story which bears on itself the stamp of truth; the details harmonize so perfectly with the local conditions of the southern delta that only here could the tale have originated. Floods arising from various causes are common in Lower Mesopotamia, and it only re-

quires just such a combination of these causes
acting simultaneously as is actually described in
the legend for an inundation to take almost the
proportions attributed to the Deluge of Noah's day.
The total destruction of the human race is of
course not involved, nor is even the total destruction of the inhabitants of the delta;—thus some at
least of the antediluvian cities survive into historic
times,—but enough damage could be done to
make a landmark in history and to define an epoch.
Its effect must have been far-reaching. The cities
which, walled and raised on artificial platforms,
resisted the flood, were the seats of the Sumerian
invaders; it was the open villages of the more bar-
barous Semitic-speaking folk that felt the full fury
of the waters, and it is probable that the depopula-
tion of the land by the Deluge assisted more than
anything else the northward advance of the
Sumerians into territory in which the Akkadians
had hitherto been supreme. Uta-Napishtim, the
Sumerian Noah, who lived at Suruppak in the
middle country and received early warning of
the rise of the waters, may have been an isolated
settler in an Akkadian district, and the 'wicked-
ness' alleged as the cause of the flood may reflect
the racial animosity between Sumerian and Semite; the instructions given to his house to 'be fruit-
ful, and multiply, and replenish the earth' were

literally fulfilled by the Sumerian occupation of the empty land.

The two dynasties, of Kish and of Erech, that come after the Flood should be more historical in character, but here again little can be made out until excavation has brought to light, as at any moment it may do, some further records to confirm or supplement the lists and legends which are all we have to-day. The most that we can gather from the king-lists is this. The Sumerians of 2000 B.C. believed, probably with reason, that the Flood interrupted but did not dislocate altogether the national life; for a period which they could not estimate but which was probably very long two city-states enjoyed in succession the suzerainty over the whole country; it would follow that the period was one of comparative peace and consequent prosperity. The third dynasty after the Flood, the First Dynasty of Ur, was founded by Mes-anni-padda, the cylinder seal of whose wife has been found at Ur. Mes-anni-padda was succeeded by his son A-anni-padda, as we know from the foundation-tablet of the temple which he built at al-'Ubaid, though owing probably to a confusion between the two names he does not figure in the king-lists, and four others of his house are recorded as ruling over Ur and, presumably, over all Sumer: with two kings proved by external evidence to be historical the whole dynasty can reasonably be accepted.

If the written records of this period are scanty and of doubtful value, the latter end of it is illustrated by archaeological discoveries which almost compensate for the silence of history. At Kish there has been unearthed part of a royal palace of the period of the dynasty of Erech; it would be rash to date the building by the most interesting single object found in its ruins, a small stone tablet engraved with an inscription in pictographic characters which must go back to a very early time, for such a thing is not easily destroyed and its presence in the debris covering the ruin might be accidental, but there is no doubt that the palace is older than the First Dynasty of Ur. The building, which covers a large area and contains many rooms arranged on an elaborate plan, is constructed of sun-dried bricks of the plano-convex type, i.e. oblong bricks with a rounded top wherein are two impressed finger-marks intended to give lodgement to the mud mortar; a monumental flight of stairs led up to the entrance, the surface of the walls is relieved by shallow panelling in the brickwork and, most surprising of all, there are colonnades with massive brick columns and brick columns support the roof of the main hall. Fragments were found of a very remarkable wall-

decoration, slabs of slate inlaid with human and
animal figures silhouetted in shell and mother-of-
pearl, pastoral scenes and scenes of victory in war
with bound captives being led before the king.
The technique of the work is admirable, but the
drawing, especially of the human figures, is primitive and the type represented is peculiar, contrasting strongly with what we have on nearly contemporary monuments from Ur: the men with long
pointed beards are presumably meant for Akkadians, but the workmanship of the plaques and the
construction of the building as a whole are purely
Sumerian. Of the kings of the First Dynasty of
Kish four have names which are apparently
Semitic, the rest Sumerian; Sumerian influence
therefore had long been prevalent so far north
as this, and though the rulers of the later Kish
dynasties seem to have been Semitic Akkadians,
Sumerian civilization dominated absolutely. This
palace of an unnamed king, who presumably was
a vassal of the Sumerian overlord of Erech, illustrates the prosperity of the country as a whole and
the high level of workmanship attained by the
artists and architects of the south.

At Ur has been found a cemetery of which the
earlier graves would seem to date to about 3500
B.C. and the latest to come down to the beginning
of the First Dynasty of Ur; amongst them are the

tombs of local kings not recorded in the king-lists. The graves of the commoners consist of a square shaft sunk in the soil and measuring on the average five feet by rather less than four; at the bottom of this the body, in the simplest type of grave, is laid wrapped in matting; sometimes the bottom of the shaft is itself lined with matting, sometimes there is a regular coffin made of matting or wattle-work strengthened with wooden uprights, and occasionally there is a coffin of wood; a distinct but contemporary type of burial has an oval coffin of clay, the ornamentation of which is derived from basket-work. The dead man is laid on his side, the legs more or less bent, the hands brought up before the face and generally holding to the lips a drinking-bowl of pottery, copper, or stone; his more personal possessions are placed with him, other offerings outside the matting roll or coffin in the free half of the shaft area. In some early graves there were apparent signs of burning, as if the upper part of the body had been partly cremated, a custom which had died out completely before the historic period; in many there is placed near or over the grave proper a model boat of bitumen charged with a cargo of clay vessels containing food. The royal graves consist of buildings in stone or brick constructed at the bottom of a shaft sunk in the soil; the walls of the building are of rough limestone, the roofs are in the form of vaults with apsidal ends, sometimes corbel-built in stone, i.e. with each course projecting beyond the one below it so as to form a 'false arch', sometimes of brick built as a true arch with radial joints; the doors in the walls of the tomb chambers were arched with brick or stone. Mud mortar was used for the construction of walls and roof, but a fine lime plaster was applied to the whole inner face of the chamber and in some cases to the floor also. It is astonishing to find that at this early period the Sumerians were acquainted with and commonly employed not only the column but the arch, the vault, and (as may be argued from the apsidal ends of the chambers) the dome, architectural forms which were not to find their way into the western world for thousands of years.

That the general level of civilization accorded with the high development of architecture is shown by the richness of the graves. Objects of gold and silver are abundant, not only personal ornaments but vessels, weapons, and even tools being made of the precious metals; copper is the metal of everyday use. Stone vases are numerous, white calcite (alabaster) being most favoured, but soapstone, diorite, and limestone also common, while as rarities we find cups or bowls of obsidian and lapis lazuli; lapis and carnelian are the stones ordinarily used by the jeweller. The inlay technique that was illustrated by the Kish wall-decoration, carried out in shell, mother-of-pearl, and lapis lazuli, occurs freely in the graves at Ur.

A description of the contents of the grave of a prince, Mes-kalam-dug, belonging to the latter part of the cemetery period, will show the wealth of this civilization. The grave was an ordinary one, a plain earth shaft, at the bottom of which was a wooden coffin containing the body with a space alongside it wherein the offerings were placed. The prince wore a complete head-dress or helmet of beaten gold in the form of a wig, the hair rendered by engraved lines and the fillet which bound it by a twisted band also engraved; the helmet came down to the nape of the neck and covered the cheeks, the ears being represented in the round and the side-whiskers in relief; it is just such a head-covering as is represented on Eannatum's Stela of the Vultures. With the body were two plain bowls and a shell-shaped lamp of gold, each inscribed with the name of the prince; a dagger with gold blade and gold-studded hilt hung from his silver belt and two axes of electrum lay by his side; his personal ornaments included a bracelet of triangular beads of gold and lapis lazuli, hundreds of other beads in the same materials, earrings and bracelets of gold and silver, a gold bull amulet and a lapis amulet in the form of a seated calf, two silver lamps shaped as shells, a gold pin with lapis head. Outside the coffin the offerings were far more numerous. The finest of them was a gold bowl, fluted and engraved, with small handles of lapis lazuli; by this lay a silver libation-jug and a patten; there were some fifty cups and bowls of silver and copper and a great number of weapons, a gold-mounted spear, daggers with hilts decorated with silver and gold, copper spears, axes and adzes, and a set of arrows with triangular flint heads.

The royal graves with masonry tomb chambers had been even richer, and these presented a feature to which there was no parallel in the plain shaft graves. The burial of the kings was accompanied by human sacrifice on a lavish scale, the bottom of the grave pit being crowded with the bodies of men and women who seemed to have been brought down here and butchered where they stood. In one grave the soldiers of the guard, wearing copper helmets and carrying spears, lie at the foot of the sloped *dromos* which led down into the grave; against the end of the tomb chamber are nine ladies of the court with elaborate golden head-dresses; in front of the entrance are drawn up two heavy four-wheeled carts with three bullocks harnessed to each, and the driver's bones lie in the carts and the grooms are by the heads of the animals; in another grave, that of Queen Shub-ad, the court ladies are in two parallel rows, at the end of which is the harpist with a harp of inlay work decorated with a calf's head in lapis and gold, and the player's arm-bones were found lying across the wreckage of the instrument; even inside the tomb chamber two bodies were found crouched, one at the head and the other at the foot of the wooden bier on which the queen lay. In no known text is there anything that hints at human sacrifice of this sort, nor had archaeology discovered any trace of such a custom or any survival of it in a later age; if, as I have suggested above, it is to be explained by the deification of the early kings, we can say that in the historic period even the greater gods demanded no such rite: its disappearance may be an argument for the high antiquity of the Ur graves.

The temple of al-'Ubaid illustrates the religious architecture of the First Dynasty of Ur. On a little mound some four miles from the city A-anni-padda built a shrine to Nin-Khursag, the Mother Goddess, which is no less surprising than the tomb furniture of the preceding period and in its way as rich. A flight of stone steps led up to the top of the platform on which the shrine stood; at the stair-head opened a porch with wooden columns overlaid with copper or with a mosaic in mother-of-pearl, black shale, and red limestone set in bitumen; the entrance was flanked by life-size heads of lions worked in copper with inlaid eyes and teeth, and above the door was a great copper relief showing the eagle-god Im-dugud grasping two antlered stags. The walls of the building, constructed in plano-convex mud brick, were adorned on the outside with copper statues of bulls modelled in the round, with a copper frieze of bulls in relief, and with two friezes of inlay work, figures in white stone or shell set against a background of black shale, the subjects of the lower frieze being cattle and scenes from pastoral life, while the upper consisted of a row of birds; clay flower rosettes with inlaid petals of red, black, and white further enriched the façade.

The discovery in the ruins of a limestone tablet inscribed in well-developed cuneiform with the dedication of the building by 'A-anni-padda king of Ur, son of Mes-anni-padda king of Ur', and of a gold bead also inscribed with the king's name and title fixes the foundation of the temple to a definite period in Sumerian history and proves that thus far back at least the king-lists rest on a basis of solid fact; the cemetery at Ur, being of considerably earlier date, should belong to the time when according to the king-lists, Erech held the suzerainty of Sumer and Ur was a vassal

state. But it is interesting to observe that between
the contents of the graves and the wall-decorations
of al-'Ubaid there can be traced no real development of style; even where, as in the case of lions'
heads worked in the round, we have earlier and
later versions of the same theme, the artistic conventions are the same and the technique has not
changed; clearly we are in the presence of a
civilization which for a long period was static.
The tomb objects taken by themselves show that
art had reached already a level which would have
been impossible without a previous history so long
that the growth of certain rigid conventions would
be easily explained. On the technical side alone,
the knowledge of metallurgy proved by the use of
alloys and the skill shown in the casting of these
alloys is remarkable and was assuredly not acquired in the course of two or three generations.
The Sumerian had a very thorough understanding
of metal, and the socketed axes, for example, which
are normal in the graves, are far in advance of
anything produced by Egyptian smiths, who for
the hafting of their weapons did not get beyond
the primitive system of tang and rivet until late in
history; whether the metal be gold, silver, electrum, or copper, the casting is without a flaw and
the design is so admirably suited to its purpose that
spear-blade, dagger, and axe become things of

beauty. The same mastery of material is shown in the more complex field of sculpture: a silver cow's head and a pair of silver heads of lionesses from the grave of Queen Shub-ad combine a dignity of conception and a delicacy of treatment which could only be attained by a craftsman whose skill of hand did justice to his imagination: even more striking perhaps is the solid-cast electrum ass which decorates the rein-ring of the queen's chariot-pole, for here there is a frank realism such as in more hackneyed subjects had been ousted by the traditions of art and at the same time a respect for material, evinced by the resolving of curves into planes, which was only recovered by the Greek masters of the fifth century B.C. If we can sometimes detect a garish element in their art, as for instance in the harps with their animal's heads in gold and lapis lazuli or in the head-dress of the queen, overweighted with rings and wreaths and flowers and ribbons of gold and beads of lapis and carnelian, this is but due to the difference between Oriental and Western taste. The Sumerian did not let colour and complexity blind him to the beauty of pure line, as is shown by the plain bowls and goblets of exquisite shape which were amongst the treasures of the graves of Shub-ad and Mes-kalam-dug, and when he does adorn such with fluting and engraving the decoration is perfectly harmonious and emphasizes the structural lines of the vessel. In the engraved shell plaques, especially those from the bull figure with gold and lapis head found in the king's grave, there is a power of composition, a sense of balance and a clean sure draughtsmanship which, quite apart from the character of the subjects, make them remarkable. So far as we know, the fourth millennium before Christ saw Sumerian art at its zenith. By the First Dynasty of Ur if there is any change it is in the nature of a decadence, and from later ages we have nothing to parallel the treasures of the prehistoric tombs. To some extent this may be owing to the accidents of survival—no royal tomb of the Third Dynasty of Ur has been found, and that great period of history is illustrated to-day by strangely few remains of its art. The principles of architecture understood by the early tomb-builders were not forgotten and the use of the vault, the arch, and the dome seems to have been continuous, and stone sculpture certainly did advance beyond the crude efforts of the First Dynasty artists, but for the rest the evidence that we have would seem to show a steady decline both in imagination and in craftsmanship. The conventions already fixed in the time of A-anni-padda gradually crushed all originality and with lack of interest the worker lost his skill also, so that when

Babylon inherited the art of Sumer we are brought up against the stereotyped and lifeless figures, smothered with meaningless ornament, of Hammurabi and the Kassite kings. But in 3500 B.C. Sumerian art stood at a level seldom reached in the ancient world, and it must have had behind it centuries of growth and experience. To this extent the excavations at Ur support the tradition latent in the fantastic chronology of the king-lists that between the Flood and the rise of the First Dynasty of Ur the lapse of time was very long.

That the rule of Mes-anni-padda extended beyond the boundaries of his own city-state over the whole of Sumer is only an inference from the king-lists, which presumably deal primarily with the suzerains of the land; he himself makes no such claim. But the contents both of the al-'Ubaid temple and of the prehistoric graves show that the civilization of Ur at that time was no localized and isolated thing. Rich as were the irrigated plains of Lower Mesopotamia, their wealth is purely agricultural; there is no metal here and no stone, and not the least interesting point about the treasures recovered from the site of Ur is that the raw material of nearly all of them is imported from abroad. Bitumen was brought down river from Hit, then Subartu land; copper came from Oman, as is shown by analysis of the ores, and probably

also from the Caucasus; silver from Bulgar Maden
in northern Cilicia and from the hills of south
Elam; gold may have been imported from Elam,
from Cappadocia, from the Khabur district and
from the Antioch region of Syria. Limestone
could be got from Jebel Simran, a hundred miles
to the south, or, for the finer qualities, from the
upper Euphrates valley; diorite was brought by
sea from Magan, some point on the Persian Gulf;
of the 'alabaster' or calcite, as it is more properly
termed, some seems to be of Persian origin, some
is stalagmitic calcite probably from cave de-
posits on the western shore of the Gulf; lapis
lazuli is said to have come from Persia where is a
mountain called by the later Assyrians 'the mountain of lapis', but it appears that there is no lapis
found there, nor any signs of ancient working; the
stone is fetched from much farther east, from the
Pamirs, and the 'mountain of lapis' is but the commercial station at which the eastern caravans
discharge and the lapis is sold and taken over by
the western traders; such trade with the far east is
entirely consistent with the existence in the Indus
valley of a civilization akin to the Sumerian and,
as is proved by the seals found in the two countries,
contemporary with that of the Ur graves and of
Mes-anni-padda. Lastly there are found in Egypt,
about the time of the First Dynasty there, which

is roughly contemporary with the First Dynasty of Ur, certain products which are unmistakably borrowed from Mesopotamia, stone mace-heads, cylinder seals, stone vase shapes and the panelled decoration of walls, and such borrowings denote at least a trade connexion with the Euphrates valley.

Trade as extensive as this could not have existed unless the civilization to which it ministered had been sufficiently widespread to afford a good market and sufficiently strong to secure safety on the roads. Evidence for this is not lacking, for there have been found at Kish graves of the same type as those at Ur; the earliest buildings at Asshur, the later capital of Assyria, are purely Sumerian, and though they are some hundreds of years later in date (they belong to about 2700 B.C.) they prove the northward extension of Sumerian culture at an early period: as far afield as the village of Hammâm on the northern frontier of Syria there have been found in Hittite graves shell cylinder seals of Sumerian workmanship dating from about 3000 B.C., and lastly at Astarabad at the south-east corner of the Caspian Sea there was discovered a treasure of gold objects which show at least the influence of Sumerian art.

Clearly then, during the period which preceded the First Dynasty of Ur, Sumerian civilization had consolidated itself and enlarged its area. It is true that even in the south country the population was mixed with a Semitic element probably derived from the western desert but perhaps containing also remnants of an earlier Akkadian occupation, but such formed only the substratum of a society absolutely dominated by the Sumerians. In the north where the Akkadians were in the numerical majority the moral ascendancy of the Sumerians was hardly less pronounced; the Semites were a more virile and a more warlike stock, but they were savages compared to the southern race and unable to stand out against its higher civilization. Such hints as we have of the political situation may reflect this cultural victory. The seat of the first postdiluvian dynasty is at Kish, in Akkad (perhaps owing to the greater havoc wrought by the Flood on the older Sumerian centres nearer to the Gulf), and four of its kings bear Semitic names; then the focus of power shifts to the south, to the purely Sumerian city of Erech, and the next change is to the south again when Ur assumes the suzerainty. Mes-anni-padda must have ruled that part of Mesopotamia which in later times was distinguished as Sumer and Akkad, and though there are no grounds for claiming for his house any wider dominion, yet both they and their predecessors of Erech must have been powerful enough to induce the neighbouring states to allow

passage to their trade caravans. As well as grain
and dates, almost the only natural products of the
country, finished articles of Sumerian manufacture
must have been exported to pay for the raw
materials coming in from abroad, and thereby the
superiority of Sumerian culture was duly adver-
tised and the way paved for further political pene-
tration; the commercial settlement at Ganes in
Cappadocia of which we hear in the time of Sargon
of Akkad had already then been long established
and its origins may well go back to the First
Dynasty, nor is there any reason to suppose that it
was the only trade colony of the sort founded in
foreign parts. Without assuming any wars of conquest beyond the boundaries of the delta kingdom,
we can picture Sumer as a powerful political unit
held together partly by force but in a greater
degree, at the present time, by the bond of a
civilization which had imposed itself uniformly on
the different elements of the population and was
exercising a profound influence on the neighbouring peoples.

In the advance of civilization the lead is generally
aken by military science and equipment. In the
case of the Sumerians, set down in the midst of
peoples physically more powerful and addicted to
war as a pastime, intellectual and artistic superiority would have made little headway, could not

indeed have held its own against the covetousness
it must have provoked, unless that genius had been
applied to war not less than to peace. They built
up an empire because they had a better army and
better weapons than their neighbours, and throughout their annals war plays a very large part. A
sketch of their military organization is therefore
desirable at this stage, even though it means that
we must to some extent anticipate history.

The materials on which such a sketch must be
based are for the fourth millennium B.C. a 'standard'
from a royal grave at Ur, the actual weapons from
the same cemetery and from the cemetery at Kish,
and the Kish inlays; for the early part of the third
millennium B.C. the stela of the Vultures set up by
Eannatum of Lagash and the stela of Naram-Sin,
both now in the Louvre; for the later period
pictorial records help us little, but we have various
notes from royal and other inscriptions and certain
clauses in the Law Code of Hammurabi.

The 'standard' of Ur is a panel of mosaic in shell
and lapis lazuli with figures arranged in three
rows; it dates from about 3500 B.C. On one side is
a scene of war. In the bottom row are chariots,
each drawn by four asses—the horse was not
known in Mesopotamia until 2000 B.C. or later.
The chariots are low-hung on four solid wheels
each made of two pieces of wood clamped together

14. THE MOSAIC 'STANDARD' AT UR

One side, showing the Sumerian army of the fourth millennium B.C.

and fixed to the axle which revolves with it; the tyres, judging from actual examples found in the graves, seem to have been of leather. The body of the car was square with a lower step at the back, lightly built with a wooden frame filled in with leather (?) panels; for the protection of the driver the front was carried up higher in two round-topped shields with between them a V-shaped depression through which passed the reins. The reins, sometimes decorated with beads of lapis and silver, went through the loops of a rein-ring fixed to the chariot-pole and were attached to the silver headstalls; there was no bit, and a broad collar of metal over wood or leather is the only other element of the harness that can be distinguished. In each chariot there was a driver and a fighting man; the weapons of the latter are light throwing-spears carried in a quiver attached to the front of the car; actual examples of these have been found in sets of four, of which two are fitted with pronged butts for use with a throwing-thong and would be discharged at a greater range, two have plain butts and are intended for in-fighting. In the middle row of the standard come the infantry. On the left are men advancing together in close order; the artist probably meant to represent a phalanx. They wear conical copper helmets with fixed cheek-pieces and chin-straps, the latter made of leather or of silver chain; they wear kilts cut in points or possibly made up of leather strips sewn to a belt, and over this long cloaks of thick heavy stuff, probably felt (or the spots on them may mean leopard's skin), such as would have afforded very fair protection to the wearer; the cloak is fastened at the neck by a toggle and hangs open down the front. The weapon of the phalanx-man is a short-handled spear. In front of the phalanx are seen men engaged in single combat with the enemy; they are armed indifferently with the axe, scimitar, or with a short spear and with a dagger, and instead of the straight heavy cloak they wear over the kilt a cloak or rather shawl of lighter stuff which passes round the waist and over the left shoulder; these are presumably the skirmishers or light infantry. In the top row the king armed with a broad-bladed spear and an adze is seen standing in front of his chariot to receive the prisoners. The grave of the Prince Mes-kalam-dug produced a remarkable head-dress in the form of a wig of beaten gold which is undoubtedly a royal helmet; on the standard, however, the king is shown wearing a plain conical helmet like that of his soldiers.

The cemetery, and the royal graves in particular, have supplied numerous examples of copper pike-heads square in section and sometimes as much as two and a half feet long; this is an arm not

represented on the standard. On the standard
again there are no archers (as there are none on
the stela of the Vultures; they appear only on the
stela of Naram-Sin, an Akkadian monument,
whence it has been argued that the bow and arrow
was not used by the early Sumerians, a conclusion
apparently supported by Dungi's statement that
in the time of the Third Dynasty of Ur he 'enrolled the sons of Ur as archers'); but in the graves
arrow-heads of many types are found and even
fragments of decorated bows; some of the former,
such as the flint heads from the grave of Mes-
kalam-dug, were not likely to have been used for
war, but others are certainly military weapons,
and we are therefore obliged to assume the existence of a force of archers in the Sumerian army of
the fourth millennium B.C.

The pear-shaped stone mace-head, a typically
Sumerian weapon which continued to be employed as a symbol of authority down to a quite
late period, had already fallen out of practical use;
in the cemetery a single example has been found of
a copper mace, a cylinder closely set with short
pointed knobs. Another weapon which may be
regarded as a survival is a scimitar-blade of thin
copper attached to a crooked wooden handle by
copper bolts and a gold band; two such were
found in the grave of Queen Shubad, and one

exactly similar is represented as carried by the king on a shell inlay from Kish. The sharp cutting adze such as is carried by the king on the Ur standard is common in the graves. No shields are represented on the mosaic, but discoveries made in the tombs seem to imply that there were already in use large rectangular shields of wood ornamented with metal bosses or with reliefs executed in copper.

In the royal graves adzes, axes and spears of gold occur; in a few other graves axes of silver; the latter may well be the insignia of officers.

By the time of Eannatum (*c.* 2800 B.C.) changes have taken place in the army. On the stela of the Vultures no force of chariots is represented and only the king is mounted in a car, this time apparently a lighter two-wheeled vehicle resembling that on a limestone stela of early but uncertain date found in the graveyard of Ur; in another register of the stela he is shown fighting on foot at the head of his men. It looks very much as if the chariot were merely for transport and not for the actual field of battle; the army is on the march with spears at the slope, not engaged with the enemy; the king is alone in his chariot and holds the reins himself, which he could hardly do if at the same time he had to make serious use of the very long and heavy spear which he holds above his head in his left hand as if pointing the way to his followers. The phalanx too has been developed; it now consists of six close ranks of men wearing the old copper helmets but armed with heavy pikes and axes, and the front-rank men carry big rectangular shields; their dress is a more elaborate form of the 'kaunakes' flounced skirt and they have discarded the protective felt cloak, leaving the body bare above the waist: the king's dress is the flounced skirt and a shawl of the same material which passes over the left shoulder and under the right arm, and he wears a wig-helmet with chignon and ears modelled in relief like the golden wig of Mes-kalam-dug at Ur. No light infantry are represented in the battle-scene, but the task of burying the dead is carried out by men, perhaps soldiers in 'undress uniform', perhaps camp-followers, who wear only a short fringed kilt open in front and carry daggers at their belts.

On the stela of Naram-Sin the costumes are of the Akkadian type, the weapons are the javelin, the battle-axe, and the bow; as is natural in mountainous country, the men are all on foot and there is no phalanx formation, the troops, symbolized by their standard-bearers, advancing in open order.

There was no regular paid army; every citizen was a potential soldier and all were liable to be called to arms. The king in person led his people to war and fought in the forefront of the battle. From the outset there must have been, as later we know there was, a permanent nucleus for this citizen army; the king presumably had a body-guard (Sargon of Agade speaks of 5,400 men who 'ate daily at his cost') and there were officials responsible for calling out the levies who probably also took command in the field; the use of the phalanx requires a certain amount of military training and discipline, and the fact that standards were carried implies that the army was made up of units or regiments which may have had a territorial or a clan basis, in either of which cases the head-men would naturally assume the command in war. Well equipped and well organized, the forces of the city-states were able to give a good account of themselves, and the wars fought by them were serious affairs by no means like the bloodless skir-mishes of Arab tribal warfare: Eannatum claims to have killed 3,600 of the men of Umma, and as he admits to having buried twenty heaps of his own dead the victory was not cheaply won; Rimush of Agade claims that in a battle against Ur and Umma he killed 8,040 of the enemy and captured 5,460, whilst for a fight with Kazallu the figures he gives are even higher, 12,650 dead and 5,864 prisoners, and though the numbers may be grossly exaggerated they surely bespeak very considerable casualties; on the other hand, a raid of Elamites against Lagash about 2750 B.C. was carried out by a force of only 600 men, but this was not a serious invasion, and the fact that only sixty of them escaped death or capture rather confirms the view that the army of a city-state was large, well equipped, and able to take the field at short notice. A victory was usually followed by a fairly whole-sale slaughter of prisoners, and those who were spared were carried off to be slaves of their conquerors or were held to ransom; the capture of a town meant its looting and destruction, and when Rim-Sin took Isin the whole of its population that escaped with their lives were scattered and the city left desolate: the ruthless character of the wars between the city-states was one of the reasons for the decay of the Sumerian power and the final disappearance of the Sumerians.

It is easy to believe that the influence of the Semites, first as rivals in war and later as masters or as predominant partners in the common state, introduced a more thorough regularization of the somewhat spasmodic military efforts of the Sumerians. The foreign conquests of Sargon of Agade must have required a standing force of more or less professional soldiers and the organization of the whole people on a war footing: under the Third Dynasty of Ur, as can be seen from contemporary documents and from the Code of Hammurabi, which reflects an earlier system, the 'army' employed for the safeguarding of the throne and for any sudden emergency such as a punitive expedition is distinct from the *levée en masse*. The regulars were recruited from, or *ex officio* formed part of, the higher rank of the citizens and by way of pay and pension received grants of land which they were compelled to cultivate under penalty of forfeiture; this land was inalienable and hereditary, its succession apparently involving on the son the same military duties as had been performed by the father; of the profits derived from it one-third was assigned to the wife or son of the holder, who looked after it during his absence on service. Presumably the soldier received his rations while with the colours—he 'ate at the king's cost'; should one be captured in war, his ransom was to be paid out of his private fortune (other than his real property) if that sufficed; in the case of a poor man his local temple became responsible for finding the money or, failing the temple, the State; he further enjoyed personal protection against the civil authorities, a necessary precaution for a man liable to be so much away from home. In return for all this he was absolutely at the king's disposal; he could not escape service when called upon and according to the letter of the law the procuring of a substitute was a capital offence; in practice exemption might sometimes be bought by payment of an *ilku* tax. The *levée en masse* applied to the middle class of the citizens, the burgher class, who were not professional soldiers; they performed camp duties and may have formed the light arm of the service. Slaves were exempt from military duty. In this later period there is no mention of chariotry or mounted troops; reference has already been made to the statement of Dungi that he 'enrolled the sons of Ur as archers'; the Third Dynasty army therefore included bowmen, as had the earlier Sumerian forces; perhaps the meaning of the phrase is that from this date the archers were normally drawn from the burgher class of non-professional soldiers, while the professionals were reserved for service in the heavy-armed phalanx where better discipline and more regular drill would be essential.

The growth of the mercenary principle had the immediate advantage that it enabled the Sumerian kings to utilize the Semitic man-power at a time when the two populations were becoming more and more mixed, and there can be no doubt that the Sumerian revival under Ur-Nammu relied largely on the employment of Akkadian recruits; of course it substituted allegiance to the king's person for the old loyalty to the city-state, and it tended to enervate that burgher class which had once been the backbone of the city but was in these days of empire relegated to a second place and seldom called upon for active service or, if called upon, might be able to avoid service by money payments. The army of the Third Dynasty was probably much superior technically to that of the fourth millennium B.C., but the Sumerian state was by so much the weaker; it was the familiar story of military specialization and mercenary service leading to national decay.

III

THE PERIOD OF CIVIL WARS

T HE first dynasty of Ur is stated to have lasted
for a hundred and seventy-seven years; unfortunately after that the evidence of the king-lists
fails us. According to them the hegemony of Ur
was succeeded by that of Awan and thereafter
come nine other dynasties about which nothing
whatsoever is known. To the kings of some of
these are attributed again reigns of fabulous length,
and the sum total of their recorded years, amount-
ing to several thousands, is vastly too great for the
interval which we know must have elapsed between the dynasties of Ur and Agade.

This does not justify us in dismissing the king-
lists altogether as mere fable. These kings probably ruled, and their names are correctly given,
but into the schematic lists there have crept two
errors, one of figures and one of arrangement.
The impossible longevity of the rulers is due either
to some system of reckoning which we do not
understand or to a scheme, astronomical or other,
to which they have been made subordinate; the
second error is due to the fact that the different
dynasties are set in order as if they were consecutive, whereas the Sumerian scribes themselves

were aware that there was between them a certain amount of overlapping and it is probable that many of them were contemporary throughout their whole length. Since the lists are supposed to deal with kings who were overlords of the whole country, it is difficult to understand why contemporary dynasties should appear in them at all, and why, if some are inserted who can at most have been only rival disputants for the hegemony, such a monarch as Eannatum of Lagash, whose dominion extended over all Sumer at least, should have been omitted. Were those histories extant of which the king-lists are an abstract, it might be seen that the compilers had a motive for what they did; or again it might become evident that they had suffered from having at their disposal only very incomplete material for history, local records giving a prejudiced and partisan view of events within a narrow sphere as they affected certain cities and from other cities no records at all. In any case it would be wrong for us to take the king-lists here at their face value; we must be content to deduce from them the vague and scanty data which alone they justify and to supplement these by the information derived from other sources.

The period was undoubtedly one of turmoil and civil war, one city-state after another competing

for the supremacy which it was either too weak
to realize or not strong enough to hold for long.
From the statement that the dynasty which succeeded that founded by Mes-anni-padda had its
seat at Awan, a city apparently situated east of the
Tigris, it might be argued that the Elamites were
now taking a hand in the game and were responsible for the downfall of Ur, and again after the
Second Dynasty of Kish it is Khamasi, another city
east of the Tigris, that imposes its rule on Sumer,
and we may suspect yet another raid by the hill-
people on the distracted valley. One thing, however, comes out clearly. The North was re-
asserting itself against the South, the Semitic element was entering into rivalry with the Sumerian.
Three times the overlordship is attributed to Kish,
once to Opis and once even to the city of Mari high
up on the Euphrates by Hit. The rulers of Mari
did at least write in Sumerian, whatever their
racial stock; the first three kings of Opis bear
Sumerian names, but the rest are Semitic, as are
the names of all the kings of the Fourth Dynasty
of Kish, and when Lugal-zaggizi of Erech rebels
against Kish and in a whirl of conquest subdues the
whole land from the Lower to the Upper Sea this
would-be founder of a Sumerian empire proclaims
his victories in the Semitic tongue. But the recru-
descence of the northerners, though it resulted in

the division of the land into two parts, the semitic-speaking Akkad and the Sumerian south, did not at all upset or even greatly modify the land's civilization. The Akkadians had absorbed all that the Sumerians had to teach them; they were now on a footing of equality with their masters in all those respects wherein they had once been so sensibly inferior, and in the process of learning they had not lost the advantage of a sterner and more virile race; if the Sumerians were worsted, it was largely with their own weapons.

Although a few names of kings, such as Mesilim of Kish, survive in independent documents to support the historical character of the king-lists, it is only late in the period of civil war that much light is thrown on the happenings in Sumer and Akkad by contemporary inscriptions or by the late Babylonian Chronicle, which undoubtedly is based on ancient sources. Their history really begins with the short-lived conquests of Lugal-zaggisi of Erech and with the rise of Sargon of Agade; what else we know is derived from the results of excavations at Tello.

A dynasty had been founded at Kish apparently by a woman named Ku-Bau, to whom later tradition assigned a very humble origin; the keeper of an inn or brothel, she had in some unexplained way risen to power and for a hundred years (so legend averred) ruled the whole country. But whatever truth there may be behind the stories of Ku-Bau, and she was a famous character in later legend, the dominion attributed to her must have been of a loose description, for it is in this period that we can follow, from the contemporary records unearthed by the French mission at Tello, the vicissitudes of the practically independent state of Lagash, whose rulers, important though they were, find no place in the canon. Seeing that the dynasty of Akshak also was contemporary with Ku-Bau, the limits of her power and the anarchy that prevailed in Mesopotamia are the more manifest.

The mounds of Tello lie on the Shatt al-Hai, the ancient course of the Tigris canalized probably by Entemena; the city of Lagash which the mounds represent never attained to the hegemony of the whole land, but throughout this period it was ruled by a house whose members assumed the title of king (*lugal*) instead of that of *patesi* or governor. The first of these, Ur-Nina (*c.* 2900 B.C.), seems to have enjoyed a peaceful reign, for his records deal with such matters only as the building of temples and the digging of canals and, though this is perhaps ominous, the fortification of his capital; three bas-reliefs preserve the portraits of the king and his family. His grandson Eannatum was on the contrary a man of war. Between Lagash and the city of Umma, lying to the north, there was an ancient quarrel which had before now broken out into open hostilities; supported by Kish, whose suzerainty it acknowledged, Umma again declared war and on his great stela of the Vultures, which is one of the glories of the Louvre, Eannatum records his victory. The *patesi* of Umma was slain and terms were imposed on Umma whereby the boundaries between the two states were fixed to the advantage of Lagash and tribute was exacted. Not content with repelling his enemies, Eannatum embarked on a war of conquest. He claims to have conquered Ur, and a tablet bearing the name of his brother Enannatum and a statue of his nephew Entemena have actually been found in the ruins of that city; Erech he claims to have captured, and Kish, while the king of Opis was beaten and driven within the walls of his own city; even Mari on the middle Euphrates is said to have fallen to his arms and Elam to have been conquered. If the boasts are even reasonably true, the king of Lagash was *de facto* lord of Sumer and Akkad, and the fact that he made benefactions to the holy city of Nippur would seem to support his boasts; but the triumph was short-lived and within a generation Umma had seized the canal which was the main source of contention between the two towns, had destroyed by fire the stela of the Vultures, and had

defeated and probably killed Enannatum. Entemena restored the position. Having defeated
Umma, he installed there a governor of his own
with orders that he should see to the control of the
irrigation so that Lagash should not be starved of
its due supply of water; but not content with that
he proceeded to make assurance doubly sure by
the construction of new canals with which an
enemy could not so easily interfere, and amongst
these seems to have been the Shatt al-Hai. It is no
wonder that the king was deified by a grateful
people and that after nearly a thousand years
statues were still set up to his godship. A splendid
silver vase engraved with the arms of Lagash is the
best-known monument bequeathed by him to
modern times.

The next ruler, Enannatum II, was the last of
his line and was succeeded by a man who had been
high priest of Ningirsu, the patron god of the city.
Extant documents make it clear that in this and
the next two reigns Lagash enjoyed a time of
peace, seeing that even the people of Umma, the
old enemy, could reside at Lagash and exercise full
religious and civil liberty; but the peace was probably enforced, for the kings of Kish seem to have
recovered their suzerainty over the south and even
to have interfered in the appointment of the
governors. It is typical of the country and the

period that material prosperity coupled with the
fact that the real seat of government was at a distance and the local authorities dependent and not
too sure of themselves led to wholesale corruption
and oppression of the poor by the rich. When at
last a strong man, Urukagina, came into power
and throwing off allegiance to Kish could pro-
claim himself king of Lagash, he, like a good many
others in other states who had risen in like fashion,
found it necessary to secure his position and win
popular support by issuing a series of enactments
intended to put a stop to the abuses which had
crushed the lower classes. Most of his reforms are
directed against extortion by the priesthood. The
high priest might no longer 'come into the garden
of a poor mother and take wood therefrom, nor
gather tax in fruit therefrom'; burial fees had become extortionate and could be reduced to less
than a fifth; the clergy and the high officials were
forbidden to share the revenues of the god between
themselves and to use the temple lands and cattle
as their own. 'If to the subject of the king a fair
ass be born and his overlord say "I will buy it"', or
'if the house of a great man adjoins the house of a
subject of the king and the great man say to him
"I will buy it"', the poor owner had the right to
refuse to sell, or, if he were willing, to say to his
overlord, 'Pay in silver as much as satisfies my

heart and my house'. It was the king's boast that 'he gave liberty to his people'.

Since he claimed the title of 'King of Lagash and Sumer', Urukagina must have extended his authority over Nippur and probably also over some of the other southern cities which had formed the kingdom of Entemena; but with the possible exception of Erech there is no evidence for this, nor do the royal inscriptions speak of any warlike exploits. The king's energy found an outlet in temple-building, and in his short reign he must have virtually rebuilt all the shrines of Lagash; the priests who suffered from his zeal for social reforms could not accuse him of lack of piety. Then, in his sixth year, the end came; the army of Umma made a sudden and unprovoked attack on Lagash, seized the city, slew the pious king, burnt the shrines he had so lately built, and carried off the image of his god Ningirsu. The disaster is commemorated in a lament written by some priest or scribe of the vanquished city and found amidst the ruins of its buildings by the French mission which excavated the mounds of Tello:

The men of Umma have set fire to the Eki-kala, they have set fire to the Antasurra,
They have carried away the silver and the precious stones.
They have shed blood in the palace of Tirash, they have shed blood in the Abzu-banda;

They have shed blood in the shrine of Enlil and in the shrine
of the Sun-god;
They have shed blood in the Akush,
They have carried away the silver and the precious stones. . . .
They have shed blood in Abzu-ega, they have set fire to the
temple of Gatum-dug;
They have carried away the silver and the precious stones
and have destroyed the statue. . . .
They have removed the grain from Ginarbaniru, from the
field of Ningirsu, all of it that was under cultivation!
The men of Umma, by the despoiling of Lagash, have
committed a sin against the god Ningirsu!
The power that is come unto them from them shall be taken
away!
Of sin on the part of Urukagina, king of Girsu, there is none.
But as for Lugal-zaggisi, patesi of Umma, may his goddess
Nidaba bear this sin upon her head!

Lugal-zaggisi, the *patesi* of Umma, followed up
his destruction of Lagash by a career of conquest
which made him master of the whole delta. The
southern cities seem to have submitted to him without any great struggle, for he adopts their patron
gods as his own; born of Nidaba the grain-goddess
of Umma he was nursed by the mother-goddess Nin-
khursag of Adab, chosen by Babbar the sun-god of
Larsa and by Sin (=Nannar) the moon-god of Ur
he bestowed on their temples, and on those of
Nippur and Erech, his royal favour, and he trans-
ported his court to Erech and made that city the
capital of his dominion. He claims to have sub-

dued the lands from the Persian Gulf to the Upper
or Mediterranean Sea, and we have no right to
doubt the claim; but it is curious that no mention
is made of any war against Kish, which lay across
the path of his advance up river and might have
been expected to oppose it, the more so as Lugal-
zaggisi had started life as a vassal of the king of
Kish and was now in open rebellion against his
suzerain. The reason would seem to be that he
was able to take advantage of internal troubles
in the capital. Sargon, a cup-bearer of Ur-Ilbaba
of Kish (or so legend states), revolted and pro-
claiming himself king set up a rival capital at the
new city of Agade; since Lugal-zaggisi seems to
have entertained friendly relations with Sargon he
may have fostered the revolt and must certainly
have welcomed the split which weakened the
Semitic state. For the Semitization of the north,
which made of it really a distinct country, and the
domination of the upstart Akkadian power over
the south had given birth to a spirit of Sumerian
nationalism. Lugal-zaggisi posed as the champion
of Sumer. There is no other explanation for the
fact that he so easily secured the submission of the
southern cities, whose politics had hitherto been
jealously individual, that he showed such deference
to their gods, and that when at last the duel came
with Agade he was followed by the governors of no

less than fifty Sumerian states. His shifting of the capital to Erech was itself a bid for nationalist support; for Umma had no traditions of empire and its elevation would only perpetuate old local rivalries, but Erech had been the seat of the oldest southern dynasty, and the title 'Lord of the province of Erech, king of the province of Ur' was a symbol of Sumerian unity.

Lugal-zaggisi's campaign to the north-west cannot have been more than a raid achieving no permanent result, for within the space of three or four years the country which he had overrun was owning allegiance not to him but to Sargon. The new king of Akkad was a remarkable man. Of no family,—he is said not to have known who was his father, whence it has been surmised that he was the son of one of the temple prostitutes,—exposed as an infant and rescued by a poor workman who brought him up as a gardener (so, in the legend, he is made to tell his own story), he became a cup-bearer in the king's service and by rebellion against his master himself mounted the throne; he found a kingdom fallen on evil days and reduced almost to the level of a city-state; he made it the capital of the greatest empire that Mesopotamia had yet known.

Sargon seems to have realized from the first that the danger-point for Akkad lay to the north.

Sumer and Akkad had formed one kingdom in the past and might again be united in spite of the racial division now so much more pronounced than formerly, and he fully intended to absorb the southern country, but he could bide his time for that. If Sumer would but keep quiet its independence did not greatly matter, and the best means to secure its keeping quiet was to strengthen himself elsewhere; to smash Lugal-zaggisi's federation might cost dear and would not repay the loss, for Sumer and Akkad would still be at the mercy of the more savage people to the north, the brunt of whose attacks must fall on Akkad, and—here was the crux—in any case they must be dependent on the northerners, for the delta had to import all its luxuries and most of its necessities through the northern territories by roads that at any moment might be cut. To be self-sufficing the kingdom had to enlarge itself. So Sargon gave Lugal-zaggisi a respite and turned his arms in other directions.

He first secured his hold on the higher Euphrates as far as Mari, then advanced north between the rivers, where Baghdad now stands, and attacked Assyria, and the ruins of Asshur seem to show that he sacked that city; from Assyria he marched east and conquered the districts of Kirkuk and Arbil and next in order the Guti, the hillmen of the Zagros range. From Der, east of Baghdad, he

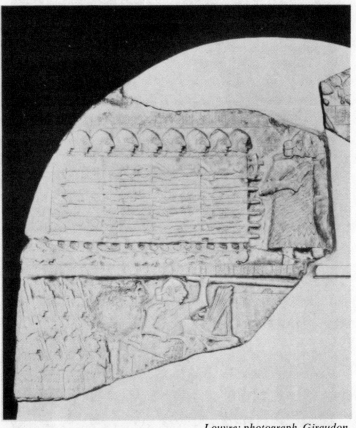

15. THE STELA OF THE VULTURES

Fragment: *above*, Eannatum advances at the head of his phalanx;
below, from his chariot he directs his army on the march

16. THE STELA OF NARAM-SIN

The King, at the head of the Akkadian army, defeats the
Lulubu in their mountains

17. STATUETTE OF A SUMERIAN RULER OF THE
EARLY PART OF THE THIRD MILLENNIUM B.C.

18. LIMESTONE RELIEF OF UR-NINA

Patesi of Lagash, *c.* 2900 B.C.

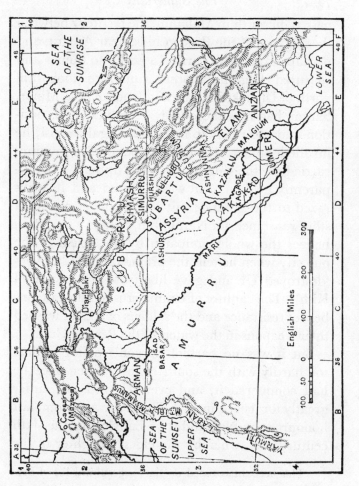

19. MAP OF WESTERN ASIA IN THE SUMERIAN AGE

From Smith, "Early History of Assyria," by permission of Chatto and Windus

passed on south to Malgium, the territory between the Tigris and the Persian hills, near Amara, and perhaps from there carried a raid into Sumer and captured Lagash; another campaign took him north of Diabekr into the highlands of Asia Minor. Sargon had now thoroughly consolidated his position and was ready to deal with Lugal-zaggisi; he invaded Sumer, defeated the national army, and carried off the king in bords to Nippur.[1] Ur apparently held out, but was captured and its walls razed to the ground; but it must have put up a stout resistance, for Naram-Sin, Sargon's son, symbolizes the whole campaign by the defeat of the one city when he tells the praises of his father who 'destroyed Ur and gave liberty to the people of Kish'. The capture of Umma crushed the last embers of resistance and the soldiers of Akkad washed their weapons in the waters of the Persian Gulf.

But it was no part of Sargon's policy to deal too hardly with the south country when once he had conquered it, and even Ur did not suffer greatly for its obstinacy. There was a custom, last honoured by Nabonidus of Babylon in the sixth century B.C., whereby the eldest daughter of the

---

[1] This account is based on the geographical list of Sargon's conquests; it certainly makes a very consistent story, but it is probably not complete and it is not always to be reconciled with other texts.

reigning king became high priestess of Nannar the moon-god, the patron deity of Ur. A limestone relief found in the temple of Nin-gal there and dating from soon after 3000 B.C. shows that the custom goes back to very early days, and an inscribed relief in alabaster from the same building gives a portrait of the Princess En-khedu-anna, Sargon's daughter, holding the same office; the king evidently was at pains to conciliate religious feeling in Sumer, and his successors followed his example in the honours which they paid to Sumerian temples. The Akkadians had borrowed the whole of their material civilization from their more advanced neighbours; what is curious is the degree to which they assimilated the religion of the Sumerians, taking over *in toto* their pantheon, their cosmology and their legends, and seldom even attempting to engraft anything Semitic on to the borrowed stock.

But their political predominance, which swelled not only the importance but the numbers of the Semitic element in the south, inevitably brought in cultural change also. Semitic names begin to appear more often amongst officials; the old Sumerian dress, though retained for ceremonial use, begins to give place for everyday wear to the northern costume consisting of a long 'chiton' or shirt, above which was a big shawl with fringed edges, carried over the left shoulder and under the right arm, while for women there was a long garment with rows of pleated or goffered flounces reaching from the neck to the ankles, and their hair too was differently dressed, long tresses braided with gold being brought across the fore- head above an oval frontlet of thin gold plate; even in such things as cylinder seals there was a notice- able change, and at Ur the great size and bold cutting of the seals distinguish at the first glance the graves of the Sargonid period. The famous stela of Naram-Sin, Sargon's son, shows Akkadian influence at work in another field. It is almost Sumerian, certainly it could not have been pro- duced but for the schooling of Sumerian sculpture, but there is something in it that is new. The pictorial freedom of the composition is in curious contrast to that orderliness which seems to charac- terize the southern art. The Sumerian might have drawn the individual figures in the same way, but he would have arranged them in formal registers, and his conventions were too set for experiment in perspective such as we have in this scene of moun- tain warfare; the innovating spirit here is that of the Semite, and that it should have found its way into the graphic arts is the most striking proof of the change that was taking place and was to end with the suppression of the Sumerian by the Semite.

Still it was essentially a Sumerian civilization and art that was diffused by the conquests afield of the Akkadian kings, and these were so far-reaching as to influence profoundly the culture of the Near East.

Having consolidated his power in and round the delta Sargon embarked on a series of foreign wars. On the east Elam submitted to him, on the west he reached the Mediterranean, overran Syria as far south as the Lebanon, and is by some supposed to have invaded the island of Cyprus. The 'King of Battle', a legend of which versions have been found at Tel el-Amarna in Egypt and at Boghazkeui in Cappadocia as well as in Mesopotamia, gives an account of a yet more adventurous expedition. Appealed to by certain Mesopotamian merchants who formed a trading colony in Cappadocia, probably at Ganes, and had been oppressed by the local native king, Sargon crosses the Taurus and carries his arms into the heart of Asia Minor; on his return he was careful to bring back specimens of foreign trees, vines, figs, and roses, for acclimatization in his own land.

There can be no doubt that the principal motive of these foreign wars was commercial, the control of the trade routes and of the sources of supply. The kings themselves make no mystery of this. Manishtusu, the second ruler of Agade after Sargon, ends a triumphal inscription describing his victories over thirty-two allied princes of southern Elam with the statement that he thereby secured the silver-mines of their land and diorite for the making of statues. The rivalry of the city-states which compelled an ambitious king to maintain something like a standing army really furthered the policy of expansion, for when there were no longer troubles at home he had at his disposal a force which needed employment and could be employed for foreign wars without dislocating the normal economy of the state. And these wars were no longer mere raids; an attempt at least was made to organize the newly-won territories as dependencies under governors either sent from the capital or chosen from some local family whose loyalty seemed sure; and the governor acted as the vassal and under the direct orders of the king of Agade. There is no reason to suppose that this was wholly an innovation, something of the sort may well have been done by earlier rulers who aspired to empire, but the wider conquests of the dynasty of Agade made the policy inevitable and the preservation of contemporary documents belonging to the period proves and illustrates its practice. For the ancient cities of Sumer conciliation was the policy of Akkad; we have seen that the daughter of Sargon became high priestess at

Ur; dedications in the temples of Ur, Nippur, and other states show that the suzerain was at pains to keep on good terms with the Sumerian gods and therefore with their local followers, and of course Sumer benefited to the full by the commercial expansion of the empire. But neither the favour of the king nor the material prosperity of the country could reconcile the Sumerians to their domination by the Semites whom they had once governed and taught; Sargon's reign ended in a general revolt of the provinces, and Sumer, under the leadership of Ur, took part in the rebellion.

Rimush, Sargon's successor, reasserted the dominion of Akkad and smote Ur, carrying off many captives; but the fact that vases have been found dedicated by him in the temple of Nannar in that city shows that when once the rebellion was crushed the king returned to a policy of conciliation. Both he and the next king, Manishtusu, were mostly occupied with wars against Elam and the north-eastern states; Rimush's vases at Ur are taken 'from the spoil of the city of Susa', and at Susa was found part of a stone statuette of the king dedicated there by a *patesi* whom he had installed for the government of Elam, and the Manishtusu records victories over Anshan (the province of Susa) as well as over the thirty-two kings of the southern country. But Naram-Sin on his accession was also faced with a Sumerian revolt, headed this time by Kish under Ipkhur-Kish; it is remarkable that as well as such a thoroughly Sumerian city as Erech there were involved in the rebellion Sippar and other Akkadian towns wherein one would not suspect Sumerian nationalism. Naram-Sin not only put down this domestic revolt, but proceeded in the course of his long reign of over fifty years to extend the dominion of Agade to the farthest limits it had known in the days of Sargon. His famous stela records a victory over Lulubu, in the Zagros mountains east of the Tigris, a people neither Sumerian nor of the Semitic stock of Agade but, as an inscription at Seripul shows, practising the Sumerian religion, a proof of the extent to which Sumerian culture was spread by the arms of Akkad. At Pir Hussen near Diabekir a rock carving commemorates his conquest of the region, and inscriptions found at Lagash describe him as 'the smiter of Armanu and Ibla', that is, of north Syria and the Lebanon; he conquered Elam and invaded Magan, the district whence came fine stone for statues, situated probably on the west coast of the Persian Gulf, and like Sargon he invaded Cappadocia: 'the four regions bowed before him'.

In spite of the trouble which he had experienced in Sumer, the government of the south country was entrusted to officials the names of many of whom show them to have been Sumerians and the cities enjoyed a considerable degree of local independence, so much so that Lugal-ushumgal, *patesi* of Lagash, while acknowledging the suzerainty of Agade, yet ventures to date documents by the years of his own tenure of office; at the same time he sends to Agade heavy tribute in grain, sheep and cattle, gold and silver, salt and fish, and workmen had to be supplied for *corvée* in the capital: the religious pre-eminence of the south was shown by the fact that in accordance with the precedent set by Sargon the granddaughter of Naram-Sin was installed in the Moon-god's temple at Ur, and the king was active in the work of rebuilding and repairing Sumerian temples at Nippur, for instance, at Adab and Sippar. Sumerian tradition also justified the deification of the ruler, and contemporary inscriptions of Naram-Sin almost invariably give him the title of god.

In the reign of Shargalisharri, Naram-Sin's successor, fresh troubles broke out in the north and east and twice there are references to wars with Gutium wherein no victory is claimed. After his time the storm burst in earnest, the Guti invaded the river-land, and the empire built up by Sargon's house crumbled ignominiously: a feeble line of kings maintained a purely local rule at Agade,

Erech for a time boasted an independence confined to narrow limits, but the country as a
whole was overrun by the northern barbarians
'who knew not kingship', and the Sumerian scribes
wrote in their dynastic lists after the name of
Shargalisharri the despairing note: 'Who was
king, who was not king?' A period of complete
anarchy seems to have followed the invasion, and
there are no records to fill in the historical gap;
but in time the Guti set up kings of their own
whose control, however exercised, did certainly
extend over the entire delta.

It is to the credit of the Sumerian civilization
that it survived unhurt the disaster which put an
end to the political organization of the country.
Doubtless Akkad, which bore the first brunt of the
Guti invasion, suffered most material damage, but
Sumer also must have been completely devastated
by 'the pest'. The temple hymns bewail the viola-
tion wrought by the Guti in the shrines of Nippur,
Adab, Erech, and Kesh, and if the accident of time
has preserved no records dealing with the destruction of other Sumerian cities the silence is none the
less eloquent; during the Guti period of 125 years
business documents and works of art are alike
lacking. Yet of Sumer too it might be said that
capta ferum victorem cepit, and before long the Guti
kings were dedicating their offerings in the temples

of the Sumerian gods which the first invaders had despoiled, Sumerians were installed as *patesis* or governors in the cities—the Guti, one must suppose, were ill equipped for such complicated administrative posts—and the foreign trade on which the country so absolutely depended recovered its old importance and extension. As the conquerors assimilated, or were assimilated by, Sumerian civilization, the city-states were allowed to regain no small measure of autonomy; the excavations at Lagash have shown what prosperity might be enjoyed by one of them under a line of active native rulers towards the close of the Guti period.

Ur-Bau, the first of these Lagash *patesis* whose works survive, was a great builder of temples and in the shrine which he put up to Ningirsu he dedicated a diorite statue of himself, now in the Louvre; the fact that he could do this and that his successors used their own series of year-dates proves that only a loose control was exercised over the city by the Guti suzerain. A later ruler, Gudea, whose long period of governorship dates to about 2400 B.C., is one of the great figures in Sumerian history. The very numerous records of him that survive are almost all concerned with commerce and with temple building; one only deals with a war and that merely the repulse of a raid by the

Elamites of Anshan. It is clear that the country was under the rule of the Guti and that military campaigns were outside the scope of the subordinate city governors, but it is equally clear that there was internal peace and prosperity. The trade routes were open and commerce with foreign lands went on as freely as in the great days of Sargon of Akkad; Gudea describes the sources from which were derived the materials used by him in the building of his temples, and they cover all the countries neighbouring to Mesopotamia, from Elam to the Mediterranean, from the Persian Gulf to the Taurus mountains; and if the royal inscriptions testify to an international organization very efficient in its working, the many private business documents of the period prove that internal trade too was unhampered and flourishing. But it is as a patron of the arts that Gudea chiefly claims our respect. Eighteen statues of him are still in existence, all dedicated by him in his temples at Lagash; in one of them the ruler is represented as an architect seated and holding on his knees a tablet inscribed with the ground-plan of a temple. Sculpture in the round has made a noteworthy advance since the days of Entemena. It is true that the proportions of the body are still squat and heavy—a fault most obvious in the larger works and perhaps in some measure due to

the material; diorite was imported in the shape of
natural boulders, seldom very large, and the artist,
anxious to emphasize the most important feature of
his subject, might be tempted to make the head too
big for the body whose size was conditioned by the
block; but though the forms may be heavy and
the attitudes are conventionally stiff, there is in the
treatment of the flesh a quality that fully atones
for this. The musculature is faithfully observed,
but rendered without any of that harsh exaggeration which disfigures later Assyrian art; having
achieved strength by his main lines, the sculptor
indulges in a modelling which by contrast might
be thought almost morbidly delicate; probably in
this too he is being true to nature, and in these
figures, where underlying force seems belied by
softness of texture, exposes the tragedy of the
Sumerian. It is curious that he cares not at all for
drapery, and represents dress as a sheath which
has no particular beauty of its own and betrays
nothing of the body it envelops: it must be
remembered that art here was not an end in itself
but subservient to religious ends and limited by
strict and ancient canons; the wonder is that, thus
conditioned, the artist yet attains to such a degree
of beauty and truth.

Ever since de Sarzec's discovery of the first
twelve statues at Tello they and the fragments of

bas-reliefs which were found with them have been regarded as the criterion of Sumerian art and the Gudea period as illustrating best the purely Sumerian civilization. None the less, in the business tablets from Tello, Semitic names occur freely and even in the religious texts Semitic phrases are introduced; it is clear that so far south as Lagash the population was becoming more and more mixed, and the racial element which was strong enough to gain a footing of equality with the old—and once hostile—Sumerian people was likely to be strong enough also to submerge them. Sumerian civilization had imposed itself first on the Akkadians, then on the Guti, and had pursued its own course of development uninfluenced by its proselytes, but the political individuality of the south country was being steadily undermined.

The process must have been obvious at the time and have wakened the resentment of the Sumerians, who would not without a struggle relinquish their traditional superiority. Gudea's records are curiously silent as to politics, so silent that the chronology of his period is a matter of conjecture—there is no mention of any Guti overlord, no reference to the *patesis* of other towns which might help to synchronize events, but there can be little doubt that he lived to see the end of the Guti tyranny. And this end was a Sumerian renaissance. Utu-

20. CYLINDER SEALS

1. Cylinder seal (lapis lazuli) of Nin-dumu-Nin, wife of Mes-anni-padda, founder of the First Dynasty of Ur. 2. Cylinder seal (lapis lazuli) of Queen Shub-ad. 3. Cylinder seal of a servant of the daughter of King Sargon of Akkad

(see page 89)

21. STATUE OF UR-NINGIRSU, SON OF GUDEA,
Patesi OF LAGASH

khegal, the *patesi* of Erech, revolted against 'the enemy of the gods' and proclaimed the independence of Sumer; it is symptomatic that in his proclamation the name Sumer occurs for the first time as that of the united south land. Tirigan, the Guti king, attempted a compromise, sending as envoys to Erech two men, a Sumerian and a Semite—and his choice of the latter further shows how important had become the Semitic population of the south—but the embassy failed. In the battle that followed Tirigan was abandoned by his own troops and, made prisoner by the people of the village of Dubrum, was handed over to Utu-khegal, and the forces of the Guti were finally expelled from the land. Utu-khegal assumed the title of king, appointed native governors to the various cities, and under a Sumerian dynasty revived or carried on the imperial organization of Sargon.

21A. CYLINDER SEAL OF GUDEA OF LAGASH
cf. Plate 20

IV

BEFORE dealing with the political revival of
Sumer under the Third Dynasty of Ur we may
turn aside to examine the social organism which
had been growing up in southern Mesopotamia
and was to be stereotyped by the legislation of a
more settled age. Sometimes it is possible to trace
that growth or to illustrate earlier phases of it, but
very often customs undoubtedly old come to light
for the first time in documents of relatively late
date, and in so far as these are quoted the following
chapter is an anticipation of events. Since, however, it is the life and thought of a people that give
value to its history the description of them ought
not to be postponed until the history is ended; here
it will serve as an introduction to the last but the
most glorious age of Sumer, the real greatness of
which it would otherwise be hard to understand.

The period of the wars of the city-states which
elapsed between the downfall of the First Dynasty
of Ur and the Sumerian revival under Utu-khegal
saw the evolution and development of civil law.
That this should result from the anarchy of the
times may sound paradoxical, but it has already
been remarked that when anarchy led to the

oppression of the many by the few the best policy of an individual pretender to power was to conciliate the bulk of his subjects by the reform of abuses and the re-enforcement of law. The famous code of Hammurabi of which the text, discovered at Susa, is now in the Louvre, was drawn up about 1900 B.C. by a Semitic ruler after Sumer had ceased to exist, but it throws no little light on the period with which we are concerned. It is of course not a series of arbitrary enactments invented by the Babylonian king but a redaction of old partial or local codes and of old customs, and the tradition which it embodies was, like nearly everything else in Babylonian civilization, derived directly from the Sumerians. Nor was this the first time that an imperial code had been drawn up. Dungi, king of Ur in the Third Dynasty, was the author of a code on which Hammurabi's was more immediately based, and before his time there existed others such as that of Urakagina. The kings of Isin had codified the law, and there were collections known as 'the laws of Nisaba and Hani' which may date from their time; of these fragments were found at Nippur and at Erech. Moreover, every city had its inheritance of law, founded largely on decisions of the courts and so corresponding more or less to our Common Law, and these were either incorporated by Hammurabi or

not superseded by him; thus in deciding a legal
case the judges of his time could give as their
ruling that 'the law of the citizens of Sippar shall
be the law applied to the parties'. The only arbitrary feature in Hammurabi's code is the application to the whole empire of laws whose origin had
been local and their vogue restricted; the extension
of their scope made possible and sometimes inevitable certain modifications which would better
recommend them to a wider public and, in view of
the fact that the Sumerians had now been swamped
by the Semites, the modifications are inspired by
and appeal to the Semitic spirit. Comparing what
exists of the old Sumerian codes with that of
Hammurabi, we see that the tendency of the Semite
has been to exact severer penalties for certain
offences, especially for offences against the sacred-
ness of the family tie; adultery involves death for
both guilty parties, whereas under the Sumerian
law it did not necessarily mean even divorce; the
harbouring of the runaway slave belonging to the
palace or to a free citizen was a capital offence,
whereas in Sumer it was atoned by restitution in
kind or by a fine of twenty-five shekels; a slave
who disputed his master's rights over him had his
ear cut off, according to Hammurabi's code, by
Sumerian law was simply sold; but allowing for
such sharpening of penalties we can derive from

the Babylonian code a very fair idea of the law which the Sumerians had evolved and under which their highly-organized civilization flourished. The actual working of the laws can to some extent be followed from the numerous private tablets recording legal decisions, contracts, business affairs, &c. Practically every act of civil life, of buying and selling, loans, contracts, legacies, adoption, marriage, divorce, was a matter of law and as such was duly recorded in writing and confirmed by the seals of witnesses. A dispute in any such subject required the production in court of the original documents, and though the written evidence might be supplemented and sometimes had to be replaced by verbal evidence given on oath, yet for the transaction to be really legal 'the tablet' was essential. There were two kinds of court, civil and ecclesiastical, for every temple was a place of justice and every priest was entitled to pronounce judgements, but there were also regular judges appointed by the king, and certain of the higher officials such as the mayor of the city and the *patesi* or *ishakku*, the governor of the province, possessed judicial functions; in all cases the ultimate appeal was to the king's person.

The plaintiff made his first application to a functionary called the *mashkim* who was not properly a magistrate but rather an arbitrator and whose duty it was to attempt to settle the case by arrangement between the parties without regular process of law. If his efforts failed, or if the case was too important to lie within his province, recourse was had to the regular court presided over by professional judges, called *dikud*, two to four in number, the *mashkim* being associated with them on the bench. The two principals and the witnesses gave their testimony on oath 'by the name of the king' and precedents were quoted to support the judgement. A judge was forbidden to reverse his sentence when once that had been recorded in writing, and the penalty for so doing was a fine and dismissal from office, but the finding could be upset on appeal to the higher court. Constables attached to the court under the judges' orders would see to the execution of sentence; in the majority of cases this would take the form of a fine or confiscation of property, but in cases of assault and injury to the person the rule of 'an eye for an eye and a tooth for a tooth' was prescribed and was presumably carried out by officials of the government; the capital penalty was not uncommon for serious offences and mutilation was ordered for certain crimes, not only as a retaliatory measure. In every action the sentence had to be recorded in writing; the court scribe drew up a tablet in concise form, entering the special features of the case, the

names of principals and witnesses, and the result
of the trial, and this tablet was authenticated by
the seals of the interested parties, was filed in the
archives of the court or temple, and served as a
precedent for the future: sometimes it was enclosed in a clay envelope on which a summary of
the case was written and the seals of the witnesses
impressed. It is evident that in ancient Sumer
justice was put within the reach of every man, and
a litigious public took full advantage of the facilities
given them; by assigning heavy penalties for false
evidence and by granting free right of appeal the
State did its best to check the abuse of the courts.

But men were not all equal before the law. The
Code of Hammurabi recognized certain social
grades which, if we have the first clear definition
of them only so late as 1900 B.C., had existed
earlier and may well have been a legacy from
primitive ages. The population of the country was
divided into three classes; the patrician order
(*amelu*) included all government officials, priests,
and soldiers of the regular army; the burgher class
(*mushkinu*), merchants and shopkeepers, school-
masters, labourers, farmers, and artisans, were
free men but inferior to the first; at the bottom of
the scale came the slaves who, whether captured in
war, purchased, or born in the house, were legally
little more than chattels of their masters. Between

these classes the law made a very sharp distinction. An offence committed against an *amelu* was punished with far more severity than if the sufferer had belonged to the second order in the state; the accidental killing of a nobleman involved a fine of half a mina and that of a burgher a fine of a third of a mina only; if a blow dealt to the daughter of a nobleman caused a miscarriage, the punishment was ten shekels as against five in the case of a burgher's daughter, and if it caused death the aggressor's daughter would be put to death in the first case whereas to a burgher he would pay only a half-mina of silver. On the other hand, where an *amelu* was the aggressor in such affairs of violence he was punished more severely than was his social inferior, and the principle of 'an eye for an eye and a tooth for a tooth' was applied to him where a *mushkinu* escaped with a money fine; further, he paid for his superior status in other ways and the medical fees chargeable to a nobleman were double those to which the burgher was legally liable. It has been suggested that this class distinction is ultimately one of race, the aristocracy representing a conquering and the middle class a subjugated people, and it is of course true that the ranks of the latter were constantly reinforced by the enfranchisement of slaves who were often of different stock; but it would be difficult to explain why a conquering race imposed on themselves the disabilities from which the *amelu* actually suffered, and as a matter of fact the Sumerian aristocracy did not form a close racial corporation in that men with Semitic names are constantly found holding offices which carried with them the rank of nobility. I think it more likely that the caste system was in its origin military. Slaves were not employed in war, naturally, because once armed they would be a danger to the state. The *mushkinu* were liable to the *levée en masse* and might be sent on campaign as camp-followers or transport-workers and perhaps as light-armed troops, and they would be called upon to defend their own homes when invasion threatened. But the *amelu* filled the ranks of the regular army and were the backbone of the State; as such their lives were of more value than those of the non-combatant citizen and they merited the privileges they fought for; but because the efficiency of the army depended on its discipline, offences committed by them were regarded more seriously and punished more severely than those of other men: it is noteworthy that the law differentiates between *amelu* and *mushkinu* only in such matters as affect the person, where the value of the individual as such comes into question; where property is concerned, as in the case of theft, the two classes are on exactly the same footing.

Though the slave was so much the property of his master that the fine for the killing or maiming of one was payable not to him but to his owner, yet the law did not leave him altogether without rights. He could protest against his own sale and submit the matter to the courts; he could give evidence, own property, engage in business in his own name, borrow money, and buy his freedom; liberty whether purchased by himself or granted by his master with the proper formula of enfranchisement was final and beyond dispute. On the other hand, he might be branded and flogged, had little or no protection against bad treatment, and was punished severely if he attempted to escape; for a man to give asylum to a run-away slave was a serious offence and he had to make restitution of a slave to the defrauded owner or pay a fine of twenty-five shekels of silver.

The methods by which slaves were recruited and the possibility, always open, of enfranchisement resulted in there being no real stigma attached to the status; it was a man's misfortune that reduced him to servitude, not his fault. Prisoners of war, who might be Sumerians of good family from a neighbouring state and were liable to be ransomed at any moment, would hardly form a despised class, and even in the case of real foreigners there was not that degree of difference between them and their masters which enabled an American slave-owner to regard his negroes as outside the pale of humanity, nor had the Sumerian that racial exclusiveness which made the ancient Greek look upon 'barbarians' as natural slaves. The view of slavery as an accident and not an axiom accounts for certain Sumerian customs which at first sight appear inexplicably callous: not only was the free-born citizen punished for certain offences by being reduced to slavery, as when an adopted son repudiated his foster-parents, but a man and wife might legally sell their own child as a slave, and in payment of debt a man might hand over his wife, his son, or daughter to his creditor to be his slave for the space of three years. The same view caused the gulf between bondman and free to be bridged in a converse manner; if a freeman took a slave as his concubine and had children by her, she might not be sold, and on his death both she and her children were automatically enfranchised though without a specific act of adoption they were not his heirs; and if a free woman married a slave (as she could do without disgrace), the children inherited the mother's freedom and on their father's death half his property came to them and only half reverted to his owner. In a society where the free man may become a slave and the slave may acquire his freedom slaves are not likely to be ill-treated; amongst the Sumerians slavery must have been of a mild type contrasting well with the practice of many other lands where it has been instituted.

One of the criteria by which a society can fairly be judged is the position which it accords to women. In Sumer monogamy was the law of the land, and though in practice this was modified by the toleration of concubinage, yet the status of the legitimate wife was so well protected that the principle was not seriously impugned.

Marriage was arranged by the elders of the families and the betrothal was signalized by the presentation from the bridegroom to his future father-in-law of a money gift, which he forfeited if he broke off the engagement and could recover twofold if the bride changed her mind; this was a survival of an older custom of marriage by purchase, retained in order to make the betrothal more binding. Probably there was more freedom of intercourse between young people of both sexes than the practice of 'arranged marriages' suggests; a man who seduced a girl was obliged to ask her of her parents in marriage, and a betrothed girl might before marriage take up her abode in the house of her future father-in-law, and her freedom after marriage appears inconsistent with any strict cloistering in youth. The wedding ceremony seems to have consisted simply in the writing and sealing of the tablet—the 'marriage lines'—wherein the position of the two parties was clearly defined and the penalty for infidelity and the conditions for divorce detailed beforehand.

On marriage the bride assumed possession of the betrothal-gifts and further brought to her new home a dowry given by her own relations; this was her inalienable property which on her death she could bequeath to her children, failing which it reverted to her father's house, but for the time being it was held jointly with her husband. A special clause in the marriage contract could secure the wife against the creditors with whom her husband might be involved previous to the wedding, and in no case could he dispose of their joint property without her consent, but for debts contracted during married life both parties were jointly responsible. She could keep and dispose of her own slaves and engage independently in business, as could an unmarried woman, she could give witness in a court of law, and in the event of her husband's absence she administered his estate unless there was a grown-up son to undertake the task. If her husband died, she inherited the same share of his property as did each of his children and could marry again at pleasure, taking with her her original dowry but relinquishing her share of her late husband's estate; over the children she enjoyed equal rights with their father and could disinherit an undutiful son and even have him branded and expelled from the city. On the other hand, she suffered certain disabilities as against the man. A husband could under certain conditions sell his wife, and he could hand her over as a slave for three years in payment of debt; he could (unless she were protected by a special clause of the marriage contract) divorce her on very slight grounds, whereas for her divorce was a much more difficult matter and was only possible if her own conduct had been above reproach; adultery by the woman, in early days a venial offence, was more and more seriously regarded as time went on and by the period of the Third Dynasty of Ur was punishable with death by drowning. Moreover, her position in the house was rendered precarious by the imperious demand of the peoples of the Near East for children to carry on the name; barrenness, if it did not dissolve the marriage tie, at least deprived the wife of her exclusive rights in wedlock.

A barren wife could be divorced, taking back her dowry and receiving a sum of money by way of compensation; otherwise the husband could take a second wife, but in that case he not only continued to be responsible for the maintenance of the first but had to safeguard her position in the home; the new wife was legitimate, but not the equal of the old, and a written contract defined the degree of her subservience, thus she might be obliged 'to wash the feet of the first and to carry her chair to the temple of the god'. In practice, however, the status of the two women must have been somewhat anomalous, and to forestall this the wife might present to her husband one of her own slaves as a concubine; on giving birth to a child the slave-woman automatically became free (which was not the case if the husband took one of his own slaves into his harem) but was by no means the equal of her old mistress; indeed, should she rashly aim at becoming her rival, the mistress could reduce her again to slavery and sell her or otherwise get rid of her from the house;—the history of Abraham, Sarah and Hagar is an illustration of this, for in every detail Abraham was not acting weakly or arbitrarily but was putting into practice the old Sumerian law in which he had been brought up. A man who had thus received a second wife from the hands of his first could not bring another woman into his house; should the introduction of a secondary wife displease the first, she could withdraw to her father's house taking her dowry with her; but though such alleviations were provided, it is evident that in marriage the personality of the wife was subordinate to her function as mother: if

childlessness were due not to physical inability but
to the wife's refusal of conjugal relations, she was
thrown into the water and drowned.

By Sumerian law children were absolutely under
the authority of their parents who might at will
disinherit or disown them, the domestic sentence
involving banishment from the city; they could
also be sold into slavery or temporarily sur-
rendered as slaves in payment of debt; the parents
could in their lifetime make benefactions outside
the family which would lessen or annul their
children's inheritance. But in the normal course of
events a man's property descended to his children,
and the division of it among them was fixed by
law: there was no privilege of primogeniture, but
after a sum had been set aside to provide bride-
purchase money for the sons not yet of age the
remainder of the estate was apportioned on the
scale of one part to the widow and to each son, this
being in fee simple, the interest in one part to each
daughter who had not received a dowry, the principal ultimately reverting to her brothers, a life
interest in one part to a daughter who had become
a lay sister, and a third of a part for a daughter who
had become a temple prostitute: there was, however, an old custom recognized by the Sumerian
'Law of Nisaba and Hani' whereby a son had the
right to claim his share of the inheritance during

his father's lifetime (a custom which persisted long amongst the Jews, as witness the Parable of the Prodigal Son); the advance would be recorded in legal form and he would have no further claim on his father's estate. The mother's dowry was divided equally among all her children.

Besides the recognition of children whom he might have by a concubine—and these even when legitimated remained in a position of inferiority as against the sons of the true wife—adoption of unrelated children was very common. A deed had to be drawn up securing the position of the child *vis-à-vis* children who had been or might be born to the foster-parent, giving it absolute equality with them; should he at any time wish to rid himself of the adopted child, he could repudiate him, but the child had a right to one-third of the movable property of the house; did the son deny his foster-father and, having discovered his real parents, attempt to return to them, he was branded and sold as a slave, and if the mother were of the prostitute class his tongue was cut out. It may well be that the prevalence of adoption was in a large measure the result of the practice of temple prostitution and that it was encouraged and safeguarded by the law as being one way out of the social difficulty arising from the number of children whose fathers were not to be known and who otherwise would have been a burden on the temple revenues.

Side by side with a domestic life so carefully regulated by laws which on the whole are liberal and tend to uphold the rights of the individual so far as those do not conflict with the superior claims of the family, there existed a system of religious prostitution. Attached to every temple there was a body of women who formed part of the god's household, since by the anthropomorphic beliefs of the time he was credited with human needs and his temple and its servants were but a replica of the palace and following of an earthly king: the chief of these women was the bride of the deity, the rest were his concubines and his domestics; as such they were members of a religious profession dedicated to the divine service and entitled to the respect of the law. When a man entered his daughter for this honourable profession the initiating ceremony was celebrated with sacrifice and he brought with her to the temple the dowry which was required by her marriage with God; but the votaress was not vowed to virginity. There were various grades of temple women but all were prostitutes.

The *entu*, the legitimate first wife of the god, belonged to the highest caste in her sisterhood, and of her we know little. She had to be circumspect

and correct in her life, as befitted a lady of high
rank, and it must be remembered that she might be
actually a king's daughter, as was commonly the
high priestess of Nannar at Ur—and the penalty
for an act so unseemly as that she should enter
a wine-shop was, under the law of Hammurabi,
death by burning. The priestesses of the second
caste, the *Sal-Me*, were more numerous and since
they engaged much in trade and have therefore
left behind them records in the shape of contract-
tablets more can be said about them. They lived
in the convent of the sisterhood, at least in the
early years of their service; they had children, but
by an unknown father—the child of a *Sal-Me* is
called after his mother only: she could marry a
man but was not allowed to have children by
him; for that she must give him one of her slaves
as a concubine: theoretically she was the god's
wife and the human intercourse which the fulfil-
ment of her vows imposed on her was glossed over
as a mystical marriage. Less mystery attached
to the lower orders, the *zikru* and the *kadishtu*,
who are temple harlots pure and simple (the latter
are those proscribed in Deuteronomy xxiii. 18),
though the former were sufficiently respectable to
be taken by men in marriage, while at Erech, the
seat of the licentious worship of Ishtar, there were
yet other grades lower in rank and against mar-

riage with such even the popular proverbs gave warning. There is no evidence for the existence at an early period of that custom described by Herodotus in the fifth century B.C. whereby every woman had to present herself at the temple and submit her body to a stranger before she was eligible for regular marriage, but it is certain that the temples of Sumer housed a great number of prostitutes and that religion managed to throw over the profession a cloak of honour. Perverted as it was, and the degraded ministrants of Ishtar are an extreme example of the perversion, the underlying idea must have been that of real devotion, of sacrifice; the devotee gave to the service of god the virginity which as plenty of clauses in the law prove was no less precious to the Sumerian woman than to others.

Like the medieval monasteries of Europe the temples of Sumer were the centres of education. Attached to most if not all of them there were schools where boys and girls were trained to the profession of the scribe. The writing of cuneiform, with its hundreds of signs, many of them with a multiplicity of values, was an art not to be mastered by every one, but because Sumer was essentially a commercial country, so that correspondence was large, and because by law virtually every transaction of life had to be recorded in writing, the number both of professional scribes and of private citizens who could read and write for themselves must have been great. Many 'school tablets' survive and illustrate the course of study practised in the temple classes. First there are long lists of single signs with their phonetic values for the pupil to memorize, then lists of signs grouped together in alphabetical order, and of ideograms, the signs which stood for a single word or idea and might be inserted in the text before a compound group to give its generic meaning in advance— thus the sign '*ilu*' gave warning that the following group was the name of a god, '*matu*' that it was the name of a people, and the sign for 'wood' would come before the word for 'box' or the name of a tree. Then come short sentences, the common formulae of the texts, honorific titles, and so on, and from these the pupil advanced to the grammar of the language and we find tablets giving the paradigms of verbs and the declension of nouns. By this time he was writing on his own account; on one side of a flat round tablet of soft clay the teacher wrote his 'fair copy' and the learner after studying this turned the tablet over and endeavoured to reproduce on the back of it what had been written. After grammar came mathematics, and we find tables of multiplication and division, tables for the extraction of square and cube roots, and

exercises in applied geometry—for instance, how
to calculate the area of a plot of ground of irregular
shape by squaring it off so that the total of the
complete squares included in it added to that of
the right-angled triangles which fill in its contours
gives an answer approximately correct: then there
are lists of weights and measures, and for those
whose studies had a more scholarly purpose there
are introduced towards the end of our period
dictionaries in which Sumerian and Semitic syno-
nyms are given in parallel columns. Some of the
men and women thus trained lived on in the
temples as religious scribes, making fresh copies of
the ancient texts stored in the library of the god,
preparing the 'books' for the temple services,
hymns and litanies and so on, keeping the volu-
minous business accounts of the institution and
putting on record the details of the legal actions
brought before the priestly courts; some even indulged in original research and might collect and
copy out the old inscriptions on brick or stone
which threw light upon the past history of their
own city: it is to the labours of these that we owe
most of what we have learnt concerning the life
and thought of their time.

Other students went into Government employ
or used their accomplishments in private business,
but it is probable that members of the more

specialized professions, doctors, architects, &c., kept up their connexion with the temples. Gudea, the *patesi* of Lagash in about 2400 B.C., whose office was as much a religious as a civil one, holds on one of his statues a tablet with a plan of a temple perhaps of his own design; plans of estates and of canals, of houses and towns survive and most of these would be either for government purposes or for the use of the temples, the gods being land-owners on a very large scale: a map of the world intended to illustrate the conquests of Sargon of Akkad (2700 B.C.) was presumably drawn up at the royal order, though in this case the powers of the geographer are by no means adequate to his task, but the idea of the universe which it embodies is clearly that of a school of religious thought. Medicine too was a curious mixture of surgery, herbalism, and magic, and a large part of the doctor's stock-in-trade consisted of charms to exor-cize the evil spirits which plagued the invalid; he was as much a priest or a sorcerer as a man of science. Surgical operations, based on a very limited empirical knowledge of the body, must have been hazardous and the law had to protect the public against unskilled or over-rash practi-tioners; in Hammurabi's code, which embodies regulations much older than his time, severe penal-ties are adjudged for failure and the surgeon worked at his own risk; 'if a doctor shall operate on the eye of a man with a copper lancet and that man shall lose his eye, the eye of the doctor with a copper lancet they shall put out', and if he operate on a wound and the patient die, his hand is to be cut off; one may imagine that the surgeon preferred to use charms and simples rather than the knife!

The prosperity of Sumer depended on its agriculture and on its commerce. The carefully irrigated fields produced amazing crops of barley and spelt, onions and other vegetables grew along the canal banks, and as early as 2800 B.C. the date-gardens were very extensive—a number of varieties of dates were cultivated, and the harvest afforded one of the staple foods of the people. A good deal of the land was the property of the temples and the king or governor would own his private estates; there were communal lands under collective ownership, but individual rights in land were very common and it was the rule rather than the exception for the countryman to have a small holding of his own: a certain proportion of these private possessions would be *ilku* lands granted by the king to ex-soldiers, the tenure of which was inalienable and involved the duty of military service. The possession or the transference of land was witnessed by written deeds of ownership.

The need to irrigate complicated matters because the same canal would serve many proper-
ties; for the upkeep of such all the owners of land
watered by it were collectively responsible and
could be called upon for its clearing even when
their own interests were not directly concerned,
and similarly the use of water by different owners
had to be regulated, and disputes were frequent.
A smallholder might of course cultivate his own
farm, employing labour hired by the year and
paying wages in barley, wool, beasts, and sometimes in silver; if he were a poor man and compelled to borrow for seed-corn, instruments, &c.,
perhaps mortgaging his field for the purpose, he
received legal protection against his creditors until
the harvest, and should that fail through no fault
of his own, was excused interest on the loan. Very
often land was cultivated as a speculation by an
outsider, the owner perhaps supplying seed-corn
and receiving one-half of the yield or one-third if
he had supplied nothing; in the case of an orchard
in bearing the owner's share was two-thirds of the
crop, while unplanted orchard land was let for a
term of five years, four for planting, in respect of
which no rent was paid, and one when the young
trees would first bear and owner and tenant divided
the yield equally. Failure to cultivate was severely
punished—in the case of *ilku* land held from the

Crown it involved confiscation—while a tenant would have to compensate the owner on the basis of the average yield of neighbouring farms; similarly dishonesty on the part of the tenant, such as the stealing of seed-corn, brought on him a heavy fine, and should he be unable to pay this he became a serf.

The plough was used at a very early time, though the first picture that we have of one dates only from the fourteenth century B.C.; it is furnished with a tubular seed-drill and is drawn by a yoke of oxen: after harvest the corn was piled in great heaps on the threshing-floor and round and round over it were driven ox-drawn sledges of wood with flints set in their under side so as at once to release the grain and to cut up the straw for cattle-food, the same process and carried out with the same instruments as are in use to-day. The grain was used for bread, ground to flour between flat rubbing-stones, or was parched and bruised for a kind of porridge or brewed into beer; wine was manufactured from dates as well as from grapes, and from dates was also made the thick honey-like treacle called *dibs* by the modern Arab. The cattle and goats provided milk, cheese and the sour cooking-butter beloved of the East, and the river and the canals yielded coarse fish; meat was probably then as now rather a luxury for the rich, and the poor man's diet was mainly vegetarian, though sacrifices on feast-days might relieve the monotony of his table.

Thus Sumer was self-sufficing so far as the feeding of the population was concerned, as for their clothing also. Wool was produced in abundance by the flocks scattered all over the country and flax for linen was grown, especially in the north; something has been said about the cloth-factories managed by the temples, and besides these there were plenty of workshops run by private enterprise: in the later periods Babylonian stuffs were freely exported and fetched a high price in foreign markets and it is probable that the same is true of the early period also—muslin may have been in demand thousands of years before Mosul gave its name to the fabric. But everything else had to be imported. The riches of the south country must have been largely due to the fact that its cities controlled the head of the Persian Gulf up which came the merchant vessels bringing their goods from over sea: one trade route led thence up the eastern bank of the Tigris to the north, and goods in transit for the Syrian towns passed up the Euphrates to the fords at Carchemish and so made their way south or north-west. By the same route, floated downstream in wooden boats which were broken up at their journey's end, where the timber found a ready sale, came silver and copper ore, cedar from the Lebanon, walnut-wood, lye and cystus-gum; but in the great days of Sumer the Gulf traffic must have been vastly more important than that from the north. We have the bill of lading of a ship commissioned by the temple of Nin-Gal at Ur for the Gulf trade; it had been absent for two years at Dilmun when in the eighth year of Sumu-ilum of Larsa (*c.* 2048 B.C.) it unloaded on the quay at Ur; in its cargo were gold, copper ore, ivory, precious woods, and fine stone for the making of statues and vases. These raw materials were worked up by the skilled craftsmen of Sumer and re-exported by the land routes to the west and north. The merchants of the south had their agencies or branch houses in distant towns with whom they kept up a correspondence and did business by letters of credit, or they entrusted their goods to independent commercial travellers who sold to the best advantage and had to render account on their return, receiving a share of the profits; the law dealt hardly with such as failed to keep accounts or otherwise cheated their employers, but allowance was made for loss by robbery on the road. Mention has already been made of the trading colony established at Ganes in Cappadocia early in the third millennium B.C., before the reign of Sargon of Akkad; in Syria there must have been similar colonies, and in spite of slow communications, occasional oppression by local governors and the raiding of caravans, the great houses of the east carried on their business with these distant outposts and conducted much of it on very modern lines. It must be remembered that there was no coined money and that all trade was by barter. For local dealing values were generally reckoned in barley—but for larger sums and for distant trade gold and silver were more workable standards, the shekel of silver being the unit; in the period of Sargon of Akkad gold was worth eight times its weight in silver. Sometimes, undoubtedly, the metal was handled in a recognizable form, ingots, rings, &c., which would facilitate reckoning, but even so the value had to be verified by the scales;—Abraham buying the cave at Macpelah '*weighed* . . . 400 shekels of silver, *current money with the merchant*'. The manner of doing business may be illustrated by a (later) letter from a merchant to his partner living in another city, who has sent to him one Shamash-bel-ilani with a demand-note for fourteen shekels; he writes: 'I have sent to Warad-ilishu two-thirds of a mina of silver' (1 mina = 60 shekels) 'and the receipt of that has been acknowledged in writing in the presence of my witnesses. He has gone to Assyria. . . . As concerning what thou hast written about the fourteen shekels of Shamash-bel-ilani, I have not paid him the money. Catch Warad-ilishu and make him weigh out the silver with interest more or less; from this sum take the fourteen shekels and send me the balance.'

In nearly every case a purchase had to be confirmed by a written and duly witnessed agreement, —to buy from a man's son or slave without putting the matter in writing and having a formal receipt was an offence severely punished by law: the conclusion of the bargain was signalized by the buyer giving a present over and above the agreed price, —the inevitable 'baksheesh' of the East. Women indulged in trade as freely as did men and contracts are frequently in their names. For a business system so far-reaching as that of Sumer credit was necessary and borrowing was regulated by the law; for loans of barley, that is, calculated on a basis of grain and payable in such, the maximum legal rate of interest was $33\frac{1}{3}\%$ per annum, and for silver it was 20%, but money could generally be had on easier terms than these; at Ur during the Third Dynasty the silver rate, however, rose to 25%, probably owing to the trade boom in the capital of the empire and the abnormally large profits arising from the import business. The Government too, perhaps because it was so directly interested owing to the wide possessions and business activities of the temples, which were essentially Government institutions, was always trying to fix maximum rates for the hire of houses and store-buildings, of ships, wagons and land, and to regulate the wages of the different orders of labourers and artisans; such measures could only have a temporary success, but the fact that they were made is an interesting comment on the economical problems of the time.

The Sumerian religion was polytheistic and its gods were innumerable. All of them were recognized and honoured throughout the whole land, but in every city there was one chosen to be *par excellence* the patron and the peculiar god of that city. At Babylon Marduk, at Larsa Shamash, at Ur Nannar, at Nippur Enlil, at Erech Innini or Ishtar, was the owner of the principal temple, the lord of the land, the governor of the State in time of peace and the leader of its host in war; the other gods might have their shrines in the courts of his temple or might boast lesser temples of their own, but they were little more than attendants upon his honour and offered no challenge to his supremacy. So far was he set above all others that his isolation almost defeated its own purpose; he was too great to be approached by mere man, and every man therefore would have his own tutelary god, one of the minor deities, who acted as mediator between

him and the city god and received his more
intimate and probably his more sincere devotion.

While terrifyingly aloof, the gods were at the
same time peculiarly close to man. The religion
was anthropomorphic and the gods were but men
writ large; the temples were their houses in the
city's midst, where they lived a normal human life,
eating the meats of sacrifice of which their worshippers also partook, marrying human women
and having children by them; their ceremonies
symbolized and secured the recurrence of the
seasons and the success of the crops in which, as
landlords, they were no less interested than were
men; they went to battle, and the defeat of an
enemy was not complete unless his gods were
brought as honoured captives into the palace of the
divine lord of the city. In everything they shared
the prosperity and the disasters of their worshippers:
the embodiment of the State, they rewarded virtue
and punished social wrongdoers, but their rewards
and their punishments were limited to this world.
The Sumerians had a very hazy idea about any
other life than this. For them there was no Hell
and no Paradise; the spirit of man lived after death
but at best in a ghostly and a miserable world:

> Earth is their food, their nourishment clay;
> Ghosts like birds flutter their wings there,
> On the gates and the gate-posts the dust lies undisturbed.

Such was the 'Land from which there is no return' to which a man might win if respect were
paid to his corpse; but if he were not duly buried,
if no offerings of food and drink were placed in the
grave to satisfy his needs, then his spirit must
haunt the streets and byways of this world and
vampire-like attack benighted travellers in search
of food: the offerings made to the dead were for
their comfort, but were also a protection for the
living. In this after-life the gods played no part;
man's devotion, and his prayers, aimed at temporal and material rewards; 'To Nannar his King,
Ur-Nammu for his own life has presented this' is
the usual form of dedication, and when Kudur-
Mabug restores the temple Ga-nun-makh at Ur
'for my life and the life of Warad-Sin my son' he
prays thus: 'Over my work may Nannar my King
rejoice; a decree of life, a prosperous reign, a
throne securely founded may He grant me as a
gift; the shepherd beloved of Nannar may I be,
may my days be long!'

All the gods had originally their functions. Enki
of Eridu was lord of the waters, and the god of
wisdom who invented handicrafts and the art of
writing, Enlil the lord of rain and wind, Nabu
of vegetation, Nergal of the plague, Shamash the
Sun-god of justice, Ishtar the goddess of love, and
Nin-khursag of childbirth; but the supreme god of

each city naturally tended to usurp the provinces of others and a good deal of confusion in the pantheon resulted, one deity duplicating many parts or similar functions being in different cities attributed to powers differently named: even the ancient legends might be modified to suit the local cult, and the pre-eminence given to Marduk in the story of the Creation is due to this political bias,—as Babylon became the capital of the empire its patron god Marduk had likewise to take the lead in heaven.

The great Gilgamesh Epic with the stories of the Creation and the Flood, the legend of Etana who flew to heaven, of Adapa who broke the wings of the south wind, and of Tammuz who came back from the Under-world were from the earliest times familiar and gave stock subjects for the artist, but (with the exception of the elaborated Tammuz-Adonis myth) they were not of a kind to have any moral influence on people's lives; their picturesque side might appeal to the vulgar, the learned might read into them something of philosophy, but it required the more spiritual imagination of the Semite to transform them into religion. In the Sumerian legend of the Flood the gods are angry and decide to destroy the race of man by drowning, but Enki betrays the secret to Uta-Napishtim, a good man dwelling in the village of Shuruppak on

the middle Euphrates; he comes to the reed hut
of the hero and, afraid to tell him openly, whispers
to the hut instead of to its owner,

> Reed-hut, reed-hut, wall, O wall,
> O reed-hut, hear, O wall, understand.

On the advice of the god Uta-Napishtim builds a
vessel like the 'ark' of Noah:

What I had, I loaded thereon, the whole harvest of life
I caused to embark within the vessel; all my family and
 relations,
The beasts of the field, the cattle of the field, the craftsmen,
 I made them all embark.
I entered the vessel and closed the door. . . .
When the young dawn gleamed forth
From the foundations of heaven a black cloud arose;
Adad roared in it,
Nabu and the King march in front . . .
Nergal seizeth the mast,
He goeth, Inurta leadeth the attack . . .
The tumult of Adad ascends to the skies.
All that is bright is turned into darkness,
The brother seeth the brother no more,
The folk of the skies can no longer recognize each other.
The gods feared the flood,
They fled, they climbed into the heaven of Anu,
The gods crouched like a dog on the wall, they lay down. . . .
For six days and nights
Wind and flood marched on, the hurricane subdued the
 land.
When the seventh day dawned the hurricane was abated,
 the flood

Which had waged war like an army;
The sea was stilled, the ill wind was calmed, the flood ceased.
I beheld the sea, its voice was silent
And all mankind was turned into mud!
As high as the roofs reached the swamp! . . .
I beheld the world, the horizon of sea;
Twelve measures away an island emerged;
Unto mount Nitsir came the vessel,
Mount Nitsir held the vessel and let it not budge. . . .
When the seventh day came
I sent forth a dove, I released it;
It went, the dove, it came back,
As there was no place, it came back.
I sent forth a swallow, I released it;
It went, the swallow, it came back,
As there was no place, it came back.
I sent forth a crow, I released it;
It went, the crow, and beheld the subsidence of the waters;
It eats, it splashes about, it caws, it comes not back.[1]

So Uta-Napishtim leaves his ship and on the top of
a mountain makes sacrifice to propitiate the gods,
and the gods, hungry because their food had failed
them since the drowning of the temples,

                scented the sweet savour,
And like flies the gods gathered above the sacrifice;

and decided never again to risk the destruction
of man.

    If the Flood story of the Sumerians has no par-

[1] From Delaporte, *Babylonia*, p. 207.

ticular moral, that of the Creation with its bestial brood of Chaos, its cowardly gods, its hero Marduk who enters the conflict strengthened by magic spells, creates the firmament out of the body of the slain monster and, simply in order that the gods may be fed, makes man out of clay and dragon's blood, is absolute barbarism, and the picture that it draws of the gods could in no way commend them to man's moral judgement. The fact is that throughout the religion of the Sumerians is one not of love but of fear, fear whose limits are confined to this present life, fear of Beings all-powerful, capricious, unmoral. Somehow or other virtue does appeal to the gods (that this should be so seems to be rather a necessity of human nature than an attribute of the godhead as conceived of in Sumer), but experience shows that mere virtue is not enough to engage and keep their favour; practical religion consists in the sacrifices and the ritual that placate and in the spells that bind them.

The daily sacrifices made to the god were in the nature of meals and were in fact shared by the priests and personnel of the temple; they consisted of beer, wine, milk, bread and dates and meat of all sorts; in a temple where there were several hundred persons to be fed the number of animals killed was proportionately great; on feast-days there was a special diet and those who were em-

ployed in the preparations for the ceremony were
treated to the best portions of the sacrifice. Other
rites were of the nature of sympathetic magic and
a symbolic act performed by the priests was intended to prompt the god to exercise his power in
some particular direction; thus the libations of
pure water poured into a vase containing ears of
corn and bunches of dates were meant to procure
the due amount of water for the crops. Private
sacrifices carried out in the temple were really
charms to secure an answer to prayer; bread,
sesame wine, butter and honey and salt were
placed before the statue of the god and a beast
was killed of which the god's portion was the right
leg, the kidneys and a roast, while the rest would
be shared amongst the participants in the rite.
In these cases the animal stood for the man, as the
liturgy was careful to explain—'The lamb is the
substitute for humanity; he hath given up a lamb
for his life, he hath given up the lamb's head for
the man's head'—and we have here a relic of
human sacrifice such as was actually found in the
graves of the prehistoric kings at Ur. In these
sacrifices there was so much magic and so little
religion that, in the case of a sick man praying for
health, for instance, the carcass of the victim duly
dismembered was laid on the body of the offerer
in order to purify him of his complaint. Medicine

was a well-recognized art and for every disease
there was an appropriate drug to be prescribed;
but at the same time all sickness was brought
about by the malignant spirits which thronged the
universe and preyed on men, and while the doctor
might deal with the physical symptoms the demons
must also be exorcized. Prominent in the priesthood then were the magicians whose duty it was
to conjure away evil when it came; and next to
them came the soothsayers who gave warning of
its approach and told how it might be avoided.

One form of soothsaying was closely connected
with sacrifice, for from the shape and marking of
the victim's liver the priest took his omens, con-
sulting a tablet in which all possible signs, favour-
able and unfavourable, were described; the British
Museum possesses a clay model of a liver divided
up into fifty squares in each of which is written the
omen for that particular spot (cf. Ezekiel xxi. 21).
But every kind of accident, every chance event or
unusual phenomenon had its meaning and its
bearing on the future; generations of industrious
priests made record of these, noting that such and
such a portent was followed by good happenings or
evil, and so compiled books of omens which could
be consulted for future guidance. Astrology was
one of the most important branches of the magic
art. The Sumerians had already by observation

acquired a little astronomical knowledge, and since the sun and moon and the planets were identified with gods the changes in the face of the heavens reflected the dispositions of the gods and were directly responsible for events on earth; the student of the stars therefore might hold the key of the future in his hands.

In considering the priesthood we have to remember that the Sumerian state was essentially theocratic. The god of the city was in reality its king; the human ruler, *patesi* (governor) or king, was simply his representative—the 'tenant farmer' of the god. Civil and ecclesiastical offices were not clearly distinguished. The king or governor was himself a priest, in fact in the case of the *patesi* the religious aspect was the older and in early days the more important; when Lugal-zaggisi, who in Erech was priest of Anu, conquered all Sumer by force of arms he established his claim to rule by assuming priestly functions in the temple of Enlil, and Gudea as *patesi* of Lagash performed his own sacrifices and took his own omens, and when his son Ur-Ningirsu lost his temporal power he was not stripped of his consecration as priest of Nina. The deification of the Sumerian kings only carried to its logical conclusion the theory that they ruled in the name of god. Conversely the high priest of one of the larger temples was a person of great political importance and was often chosen from the royal house. Church and State were so inextricably mingled that while the State has to be regarded as a theocracy the Church must in part at least be judged as a political institution and the state religion as a political instrument. It would be interesting to compare Sumer and Akkad under the Third Dynasty of Ur with the Roman Empire of the third century when the state worship of the gods of Rome and of the *genius* of Augustus and the city was a profession of political loyalty empty of religious content, and men, if they believed, believed in other gods. To the Sumerian the greater gods were something more than symbols, but they touched his life very lightly; the priestly magic which dealt with demons and minor deities came closer; but we shall not understand what were his real beliefs until we find out more about that domestic religion concerning which the temple texts are silent. The chapels in the private houses and the little clay figures (the *teraphim* stolen by Rachel in the story of Jacob) which we find in the ruins of the houses and in the graves may mean simply more magic brought into the home, but equally they may bear witness to a faith more intimate, more simple and more genuine than that contained in the elaborate sacrifices and set liturgies of the church.

V

THE THIRD DYNASTY OF UR

AMONGST the local governors installed by Utu-khegal was, apparently, Ur-Nammu *patesi* of Ur; on inscriptions found at Ur he makes dedications to Ningal the wife of Nannar on behalf of his suzerain. Then he revolted, conquered Erech, and by a series of victories made himself master of the whole country; the fact that Kish, the old Semitic capital, rebelled against 'the Land', i.e. against the unification of Mesopotamia under Sumerian rule, shows how truly nationalist was the king's policy; he was not merely adding one more chapter to the rather sordid history of rivalry between city-states; he was aiming deliberately at a Sumerian revival in which Ur, his native city, should take her old place as capital of the empire. From the moment of his accession and throughout his eighteen years of kingship he busied himself in making the city worthy of its position and in elevating to the front rank in the Mesopotamian pantheon the Moon-god Nannar, the patron deity of Ur; not at Ur only but in other cities, such as Lagash and Nippur, was the Moon-god honoured by new temples and public works called after his name. On the other hand, Ur-Nammu would seem

to have been content with establishing the theory
of Sumerian supremacy; in his time and in that of
his successors there was no attempt at repression
of the Semites as such, they enjoyed equal status
with the Sumerians, were eligible for all offices of
State, and Ur-Nammu's grandson, Bur-Sin, himself bore a Semitic name. Such magnanimity was
wisdom enforced. The population of the south
country was now too mixed to allow of invidious
distinctions between its elements, for a long time
the Sumerians had been steadily losing ground
and undue favouritism of them would have brought
immediate disaster; real unification was the only
statesmanlike course, and if the empire was to be
extended by foreign wars, it was the more necessary to enlist for the army soldiers of the stouter
Semitic stock. If the portraits of Gudea do indeed
represent fairly the Sumerian of his day, it is evident
that a softness and a degeneration had set in which
would have made it impossible to win or to hold
an empire by Sumerian arms alone.

To the equal treatment meted out to all his
subjects we may attribute the many encomiums of
the king's justice; 'he made justice to reign', 'wick-
edness tarried not before him', 'the righteousness
of Ur-Nammu, a treasure': 'King of Sumer and
Akkad' he called himself, and he appears to have
deserved the double title. It was in accordance

with ancient precedent that the king should be deified in his lifetime, and Ur readily fell in with the practice; but in contemporary inscriptions from other cities the divine title is never added to the king's name, and his worship seems to have been limited to his native place. It may be that inter-state jealousies were still too strong for Erech or Kish to accept the godhead of one who was primarily ruler of Ur, it may be simply that they doubted the permanence of an authority which had begun, as so many others had begun, with rebellion and might itself fall a victim to the same; time and use were needed for factious grudges to be appeased and for the benefits of the régime to win such recognition that the symbol of it might acquire more than mortal reverence; Dungi, Ur-Nammu's son, by the twelfth year of his reign was adopted by all Sumer and Akkad as a god.

We know very little of the wars of Ur-Nammu, though there must have been such; foreign lands paid him tribute and trade flourished along the international roads, and this could hardly have been without at least a show of arms, but the royal records which survive deal rather with the immense building operations undertaken by the king. At Ur he built the city wall, the great Ziggurat tower, the temples of Nannar, Ningal, and Nin-e-gal, and the royal palace; at Nippur his work was scarcely less comprehensive; at Lagash, Eridu, Umma, Larsa, and Adab he founded or restored temples; and he was no less active in that other task, indispensable in Mesopotamia, the digging of canals.

The waters of the Euphrates are so rich in silt that neglect to clean the channels will render them useless in the course of a few years; again the river may shift its bed and suddenly disorganize the whole irrigation system. Something of the kind may have happened during the period of anarchy which preceded Ur-Nammu's rise to power, for apart from his usual activity in canal building one of his inscriptions implies that the old channels had failed and that the province was suffering from drought and loss of waterways. It was characteristic of Ur-Nammu that his first thought in such a case was to propitiate the gods, and his restoration of the temple of the Moon-god Nannar was intended to avert the drought. 'For Nannar, the eldest son of Enlil his King', so runs the dedication, 'Ur-Nammu the mighty man, king of Ur, king of Sumer and Akkad, who built the temple of Nannar, gloriously restored its former state, saying "Open it!"; he saved the vegetables in the garden plot, and the ships of Magan he restored to its hand.' In the immediate neighbourhood of the capital alone at least four canals were excavated by his orders, one of them, as is implied above, connecting the city directly with the sea so that the trading-vessels of the gulf could unload on the quays of Ur; the canal of Nannar at Lagash was his work, and on his great stela found at Ur he gives a whole list of others.

It is clear that the main energies of the king were directed to the consolidation of his authority at home, and he may have been content to leave to neighbouring states their independence, at least for a while, provided that they kept the peace and respected his merchant trains. The limestone stela set up in the capital, the fragments of which have been found in the ruins, was intended to summarize in pictorial form the chief exploits of Ur-Nammu's reign, those which would most command the gratitude of his people; judging from what remains of it, 'the merciful lord who brought prosperity to Ur' deserved his title. The stone, measuring five feet across and perhaps three times as much in height, was sculptured on both sides with reliefs arranged in horizontal registers. Of the scenes only one, in which bound prisoners are led before the king, has to do with war. The top scene on either side refers to the digging of canals whose names are written below; the king is shown standing in the attitude of worship and there flies down to him from heaven an angel holding a vase from which the water of fertility is pouring out upon the ground. Another scene showed cattle and men milking them; the two staple industries of Mesopotamia, the agricultural and the pastoral, had received the protection and encouragement of the king. The remaining registers illustrate his piety towards the gods. In one there is a scene of sacrifice, animals being killed and libations poured out before an altar: in another the king himself makes his libation to Nannar and to Ningal. Here Nannar holds in his hand what appear to be the measuring-rod and line of the architect, as if commanding the king to build him an house; in the next scene below, Ur-Nammu obediently comes before the god as a workman bearing on his shoulder the tools of the builder, and on another register is shown the actual building in progress, men climbing ladders and laying the bricks of what must be the king's greatest work, the Ziggurat of Nannar at Ur. The monument is in its spirit a striking contrast to most of those whereby oriental monarchs have sought to perpetuate their memory; to turn from it to the wall-reliefs of Ashur-natsir-pal with their scenes of battles and the assault of cities, the enemy being flayed alive or impaled on the battlements, the scribes taking tally of the severed heads and hands, the captive gods being carried away from the flaming towns, is to understand at a glance the difference between the Sumerian and the Assyrian character.

Dungi, Ur-Nammu's son, who reigned for fifty-eight years, fought many wars and reduced to the status of provinces within his empire the outlying countries which his father seems to have left autonomous. Some of these, especially the states east of the Tigris, continued to give trouble throughout his reign and time after time revolts had to be put down by the royal armies; thus Lulubu was conquered no less than nine times. On the other hand, Susa, the seat of a *patesi*, remained loyal and contented,—Dungi built there a temple to the god Shushinak;—Anshan, Kazallu, and Kimash were also governed by *patesis*, but these were the only provinces east of the Tigris which could be brought into the regular organization of the empire; the more intractable states to the north had no civil governors appointed to them and may have been ruled by something more like martial law.

Most of these conquests were made in the latter half of the king's reign; his earlier years were spent in consolidating what he had inherited from his father and in carrying out a policy which emphasized the nationalist revival under the Third Dynasty. Dungi was as active a builder as had been Ur-Nammu, indeed the latter had not lived long enough to complete his programme of temple construction and there was plenty for Dungi to do even if he had not had plans of his own, but as a matter of fact his name is found on bricks and foundation-tablets throughout Sumer and Akkad. The chronicle states that Dungi 'cared greatly for the city of Eridu which is on the shore of the sea'; Eridu was traditionally the oldest city of Sumer and its temple of Ea the water-god was the most revered in all the south country, so that the king's devotion to the place may well have had a political motive. On the other hand, he laid waste the temple E-sagila at Babylon which had been rebuilt and endowed by Sargon and successive kings of Agade and was probably regarded as the religious centre of Akkad; since Dungi had nothing material to fear from Babylon, as yet a town of no military importance, and so far from being generally an iconoclast was everywhere building and restoring the temples of the Sumerian gods, at Erech and Lagash, Nippur, Adab, Maer, and did not hesitate to show honour to a foreign deity such as Shushinak of Susa, this isolated act of destruction must reflect the same nationalist policy as dictated his patronage of Eridu. But at the same time the king was perfectly ready to make use of his Semitic subjects, and we find Semitic Babylonian names amongst the governors of provinces: it would seem that while he was anxious to foster the union of

Sumer and Akkad, which indeed was essential if his empire was to endure at all, he was determined that the general colour of the union should be Sumerian.

Tablets found at Lagash throw light upon the very business-like organization of the empire. The local governors owed their appointment to the king as did also the minor officials, and though their authority in their own provinces was considerable the administration was largely directed from the central government at Ur; the *patesi* might himself have to report in person to headquarters, couriers passed frequently along the roads with instructions, and imperial officers were dispatched from Ur on special missions: incidentally this meant further organization, for not only had the roads to be kept in repair but provision had to be made for the transport and rationing of the officials passing through on business. This centralization of government tended to weaken greatly the power of the *patesis* who in the old days of hereditary office had always been potential rebels against their overlord while their quarrels amongst themselves had often led to wars between the city-states. Only in Nippur did the patesiship continue to descend from father to son, and there as a particular concession to the religious sanctity of the place; for some reason, possibly because the

cult of Nannar of Ur was not taken up by the kingdom at large with any enthusiasm, Dungi and his
son Bur-Sin after him paid especial attention to
Nippur and elevated its god Enlil to the chief place
in the Sumerian pantheon, and every province was
made to contribute to the revenues of its temple.

The raising of taxation and the dispatch of tribute to the capital and to the privileged temples
was one of the main duties of the *patesi*; since taxes
were paid in kind it was important that weights
and measures should be uniform, and Dungi established a fixed standard for the whole empire;
there was an official testing-house at Ur, placed
under the patronage of Nannar and attached to
his temple, and a number of stone weights have
been found there and elsewhere with inscriptions
testifying to their correctness and dating them to
the reign of Dungi.

The period must have been one of great prosperity. Throughout the king's whole long reign of
over fifty years Sumer and Akkad enjoyed internal
peace, foreign conquest had included within the
boundaries of the empire many of the sources of
supply of those necessary commodities which the
delta itself could not produce, the later wars were
little more than raids which may well have paid
for themselves by the booty they produced and the
slaves which they furnished for the army and for

the public works. The tablets from Lagash giving lists of the sheep, cattle and asses belonging to the temple and details concerning the administration of the temple domains prove how rich was the shrine even of a provincial town; at the great religious centre of Nippur the god Enlil possessed a sacred farm, Drehem, where there was a receiving-station for the tithes and offerings of cattle, grain, and fruit which poured in from all over the empire. Private business tablets show that commerce was no less prosperous, and the standard of life must have been higher than it ever was in later Mesopotamian history. The king had funds and labour at his disposal sufficient for the most ambitious building schemes and the outward magnificence of his reign was in full accord with eastern traditions; Bur-Sin, who succeeded him and reigned for eight years, was almost as active a builder as his father had been, and if the last two kings of the dynasty set up fewer monuments it may well be because there was little left for them to build.

From the excavations at Ur one can get some idea of what the capital of the empire was like in the palmy days of the Third Dynasty. Of the temples erected by Ur-Nammu and his descendants some survive to the present day; others were rebuilt by later kings, but in that case the ground-

plan of the original was so faithfully followed—
often indeed the foundations were the same—that
the new work may be taken as a replica of the
old and can be used indifferently to complete the
picture.

The outstanding feature of the city was the Ziggurat or staged tower. Every great town in the
land possessed a building of this type, which seems
to have been a peculiarly Sumerian invention.
One of the facts from which it is deduced that the
Sumerians were by origin a hill-people is that their
gods are often represented as standing upon mountains; it would naturally follow that in their first
home they worshipped their gods 'on high places
and on every high hill'. Coming into the alluvial
plain of southern Mesopotamia those hill-folk were
confronted with the difficulty that here were no
hills on which their rites could decently be practised. But the swampy character of the soil and
the recurrent floods had from the outset taught the
earliest settlers that their mud buildings must be
raised on platforms, natural or artificial; a combination of this necessary precaution and of the
traditional idea of a hill-temple resulted in the
Ziggurat, an artificial mountain. In so far as it
was the base on which stood a shrine, the ziggurat
was only the platform of the king's palace writ
large, just as that in its turn was a more ambitious

version of the platform of the commoner's house: in so far as it was a hill,—and the ziggurat would have a name such as 'the Mountain of God' or 'the Hill of Heaven'—it possessed a sanctity of its own and was elaborately planned so that every part and every line should have significance and symbolize the creed which it subserved. The most famous ziggurat was that of Babylon, the 'tower of Babel' of Hebrew legend, now utterly destroyed; the Ziggurat of Ur, which in plan closely resembled that of Babylon, is the best preserved in Mesopotamia.

Ur-Nammu's building, which occupied the site of an older and smaller ziggurat, is a rectangle measuring a little more than two hundred feet in length by a hundred and fifty feet in breadth and its original height was about seventy feet; the angles are orientated to the cardinal points of the compass. The whole is a solid mass of brickwork, the core of crude mud bricks, the face covered with a skin, eight feet thick, of burnt bricks set in bitumen; at regular intervals in the face there are 'weeper'-holes for draining the interior and so preventing the mid brick from swelling and bursting the outer walls. The walls, relieved by broad shallow buttresses, lean inwards with a pronounced batter which gives a fine impression of strength, and it is noteworthy that on the ground-plan the base of each wall is not a straight line but convex, from which again an idea of strength results—it is the same principle as was observed by the builders of the Parthenon. The upper terraces were curiously irregular; narrow along the long sides, they were broader at the ends of the building, so that the top stage approximated rather to the square; and at the south-east end the bottom terrace was lower than at the north-west; from it a central flight of stairs led to the shrine on the top stage. The approach was on the north-east face. Three stairways, each of a hundred steps, converged before a monumental gateway on the level of the lowest terrace, the two side staircases leant against the wall of the ziggurat, the central flight running out boldly at right angles from the building; the two angles between the staircases were filled by buttresses with sides of panelled brickwork. It is probable that both the tops of these buttresses and the terraces of the ziggurat itself were planted with trees in closer imitation of the wooded hills of the Sumerian homeland. As an architectural feat the ziggurat is remarkable. Limited by his material, the architect has dispensed with ornament and relied on mass and line. The design might easily have been both primitive and ugly, a mere superposition of cubes; as it is, while bulk predominates, all the lines, those of the sloped outer walls and the sharper slant of the stairways, lead the eye inwards and upwards to the temple which was the religious as well as the artistic crown of the whole structure. This ethical idea was emphasized by the horizontal division of the terraces which contrast with but do not interrupt the upward-converging lines; in the late period at least, when the tower was restored by Nabonidus of Babylon, but probably in Ur-Nammu's day also, the stages symbolized the divisions of the universe, the underworld, the earth, the firmament of heaven; and the approach to the House of God passes through them all.

The Ziggurat stood on a high raised terrace called E-temen-ni-il, surrounded by a double wall. Partly on this terrace and partly at its feet, below the north-east face of the Ziggurat, lay the great temple of Nannar. The shrine on the Ziggurat's summit was the holiest place of all, but it was too small to be the sole temple of so great a god and the main building had perforce to be elsewhere. The sanctuary of this lower temple stood against the north-west side of the tower, and on the lower stage stretched its wide outer court surrounded by store-chambers and offices. Since to every temple there were attached lands more or less extensive, the produce of which either belonged to the god or paid tithe to him, and since offerings in kind were brought by tenants and by worshippers alike, plenty of store space was essential and the affairs of the god had to be run on business lines. The temple officials duplicated in title and in function those of the king's palace; besides the priests proper there were ministers of the Harem, of War, of Agriculture, of Transport, of Finance, and a host of secretaries and accountants responsible for the revenues and the outgoings of the temple. To the Ga-makh, the Great Storehouse, perhaps this courtyard below the Ziggurat, the countrymen would bring their cattle, sheep and goats, their sacks of barley and rounds of cheese, clay pots of clarified butter and bales of wool; all would be checked and weighed and the scribes would give for everything a receipt made out on a clay tablet and would file a duplicate in the temple archives, while the porters would store the goods in the magazines which opened off the court.

Immediately to the south-east of the Nannar temple lay another, E-Nun-Makh, which was sacred to the same god and to his wife Nin-gal. This was a building wherein a particularly secret form of ritual must have been practised, for there was here no wide court such as characterized most shrines, but the sanctuary, a small square building containing an entrance lobby and two duplicate sets of two chambers, one for each of the deities its patrons, was hidden away in a maze of long vaulted rooms and was only approached by a narrow winding passage; certainly the public never were admitted here, and so small were the sanctuary chambers that even the officiating priests must have been few in number. Of the vaulted rooms which occupied most of the building's area some were presumably storerooms, but others, judging from the inscriptions found in them, were the quarters of the *Sal-Me* priestesses, the women of the god's harem. The head woman, the Nin-An, was the god's true wife, these others were his concubines; they might bear children, but the fathers of such would never be known; they might marry, but to their human husband they must not bear a child; they owned property of their own and carried on business in their own names,—contract tablets are often signed by the *Sal-Me* priestesses; they were rich and honoured, forming a class so different from that of the common temple prostitutes that they might boast of princesses in their ranks. It was natural that such should be housed in what was really the harem temple of the Moon-god. E-Nun-Makh was a very ancient foundation, dating back to the First Dynasty of Ur, but it had constantly been restored and had been completely rebuilt by Bur-Sin: important though it was in the religious life of the city, it can have been known to most only from the outside, and the long blank wall of it fronting on the Sacred Way had no architectural merit to draw the attention of the passer-by.

Very different was the next temple, Dublal-makh. The Sacred Way led through a double gateway into a large paved courtyard, at one end of which projected from the corner of the Ziggurat terrace a small but lofty building consisting of an inner and an outer chamber only. The outer chamber was vaulted, the inner, even at this period, may have been surmounted by a high dome; but its most arresting feature was the huge arched doorway which occupied the greater part of the width of the façade and was closed by doors elaborately adorned with silver, copper, and gold;[1] when they were open there could be seen an interior whose walls were enriched with a many-coloured incrustation: 'this house, the wonder of the land, he, Bur-Sin, built for him, he finished it splendidly, with gold, silver, lapis lazuli he adorned it'; against the back wall of the inner chamber stood the statue of Nannar.

The building had in early times been open to the sky and was really the entrance from the courtyard level to the terrace of the Ziggurat, and it never lost its name of 'the Great Gate'. Bur-Sin

[1] The decoration of the doors is only proved for a later period, but the work done then was probably a reconstruction on ancient lines.

had roofed it and the back had been walled up so that the gateway was transformed into a shrine with only small side-doors leading to the terrace; but one of its functions survived the change, for in old times the judges had sat here in the gate to give judgement and still it was called 'the Hall of Justice' and from its steps, one can suppose, the decisions of the courts were read to the public in the courtyard and received their sanction as oracles coming from the Moon-god's shrine.

Round the courtyard were more store-chambers and workrooms, and in one corner of it the house of the keeper of the business archives of the temple. Here there were found thousands of clay tablets throwing light on the various activities practised within the sacred precincts. The vast quantities of goods brought as tribute to the god and stored in his magazines were utilized for all sorts of purposes; animals had to be issued for the daily sacrifices, the priests and the temple servants required to be fed, wood or metal might be needed for repairs to the fabric, even oil for the oiling of the door-hinges would be drawn from the stores; and for everything issued the store-keeper made out an issue-voucher giving the name of the applicant, the nature and quantity of the goods required, their purpose, and the authority on which the issue was granted. Besides these maintenance

demands, inevitable in such a community as ministered to the temple, there were outgoings connected with the commercial interests of the god.
Within the temple precincts there were regular
factories where worked the women attached to
the temple. Thus the raw wool brought in by the
country people was spun and woven on the pre-
mises; the ledgers of the factory give a nominal roll
of the women, the weight of wool issued to each
at the beginning of the month, the lengths and
weights of the specimens of cloth of various qualities which she produced at the month's end (a due
allowance is made for unavoidable wastage in
the process of manufacture), and then in parallel
columns the rations issued for her maintenance
during the period, so much grain and cheese and
cooking-butter, the whole making a profit-and-
loss account for the month. In their book-keeping,
as in everything else, the Sumerians were a most
business-like people, but the particular interest of
these tablets lies in the picture that they give of the
life led in the ecclesiastical buildings of the Third
Dynasty. In one of the rooms by the courtyard
there were found the remains of a smelting-furnace
and a clay pot filled with scrap copper; here then
the temple servants were employed in melting
down metal, perhaps that brought in by the merchants of the city, into ingots for storage such as

were unearthed in another part of the building. These temples resembled less a church than a medieval monastery wherein besides the purely religious observances there went on industries of all kinds and the workshops and the schools were scarcely less important than the chapel.

From the courtyard of Dublal-makh a continuation of the Sacred Way led along the south-east wall of the Ziggurat terrace to the doors of another temple, dedicated to Nin-gal, the wife of the Moon-god. From the outside, with its enormously massive walls and its angle towers, it must have looked like a fortress rather than a religious building. Double gateways with a guard-chamber between led into the outer court of the northern of the two temples enclosed within the great wall, the court of the lesser worshippers. On to this opened a small sanctuary with a high statue-base immediately facing the door and visible from the court; on one side the paved floor sloped to a drain, the *apsu*, down which were poured the libations to the god. Behind the sanctuary lay a long narrow chamber, apparently an ablution-place, through which one passed into the inner court; from this two doors, set in an ornamental façade decorated with elaborate buttresses, led through little anterooms into the holy of holies, a long and shallow room, against the back wall of which stood the stepped altar and the benches for the statues and the sacred vessels. This temple formed one of the three sections into which the whole building was divided; the central block contained at one end the living quarters of the priests, and their graves, for they were buried beneath the floors of their houses, and at the other end a maze of winding passages, in the centre of which was the cult chapel of King Bur-Sin, the temple's founder. An older shrine of Nin-gal, the work of Ur-Nammu, seems to have occupied the site, but it was razed to the ground by his grandson to make room for his own more ambitious building; but Bur-Sin's temple was of crude mud brick, and about a hundred years after its foundation it was rebuilt in burnt brick by one Enannatum, prince of Isin and high priest of Nannar at Ur; but the new temple was a faithful reproduction of the old and Bur-Sin as first founder continued to receive his divine honours. At one end of the chapel room a tall oval-topped stela of white limestone was set up, inscribed with the king's titles and the record of the temple's building; two grey marble stelae similarly inscribed lay at its foot embedded in the bitumen covering of the floor, and round these would be grouped the symbols of power, maces and standards, with sacrificial vessels on the bench against the wall: through two doors at the other end the worshipper would pass across the room, pausing to pay his respects to the dead king.

The third section, occupying the south-eastern end of the enclosure, was a second temple of Ningal built on quite different lines from the first. The outer court was reduced to little more than a passage and led directly into the central court which was the main feature of the building. In the north corner stood a brick bitumen-proofed water-tank and beside it a low stone column whereon stood the laver or ablution-stoup, probably of metal. In the centre of the south-west side was the entrance to the sanctuary; in front of the door, almost blocking it, was the altar, probably metal-sheathed, and flanking it, against the wall, brick bases on which stood statues and inscribed stelae. Three great archways led to the sanctuary, a tiny square no deeper than the thickness of the arch, entirely filled by the brickwork of the statue-base and by the lower platform, approached by a flight of steps, whereon the priest mounted to make his oblation: between the arches were narrow vaulted chambers with brick benches against their walls; these were the subsidiary chapels to the minor deities who formed the goddess's retinue. On one side of the sanctuary was the treasury, on the other the bedroom of the goddess; behind these lay magazines (in one the great oil-jars were found

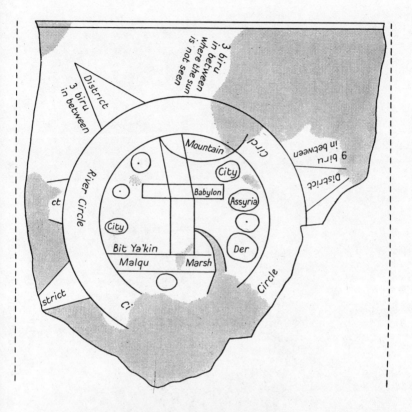

22. MAP OF THE WORLD

An attempt by a Sumerian geographer to illustrate the foreign
campaigns of Sargon of Akkad

*From Smith, "Early History of Assyria," by
permission of Dr. R. Campbell Thompson and
Messrs. Chatto and Windus*

23. THE ZIGGURAT OF UR

NE. face, showing the converging flights of stairs

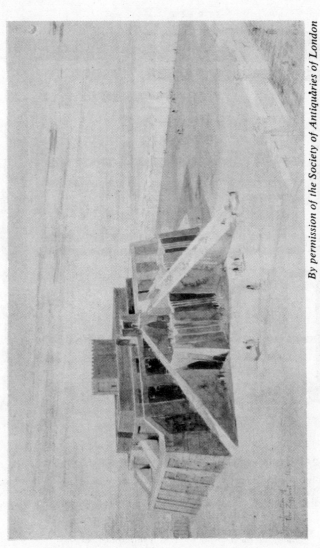

24. THE ZIGGURAT OF UR, RESTORED

From a drawing by F. G. Newton

STREET

0   5   10   15   20   25   30 METRES

25. PLAN OF THE TEMPLE OF NIN-GAL AT UR

Founded by Bur-sin, king of Ur, 2220 B.C., and re-built by Enannatum
the High Priest at Nannar and son of Lib-it-Ishtar, king of Isin, *ca.* 2080 B.C.
The building includes two separate sanctuaries of the goddess and a chapel
for the worship of Bur-sin

Based on the drawing by A. S. Whitburn, A.R.I.B.A.,
by permission of the Society of Antiquaries of London

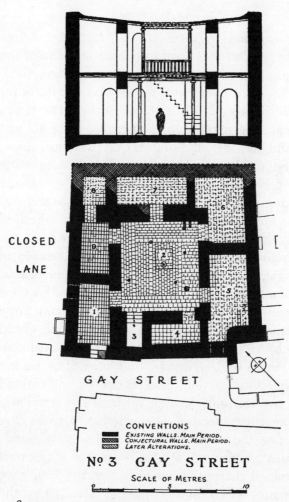

CLOSED

LANE

GAY STREET

CONVENTIONS
EXISTING WALLS. MAIN PERIOD.
CONJECTURAL WALLS. MAIN PERIOD.
LATER ALTERATIONS.

No. 3 GAY STREET

SCALE OF METRES

26. PLAN AND RECONSTRUCTION OF A PRIVATE HOUSE
AT UR, OF THE PERIOD OF THE ISIN AND LARSA
DYNASTIES

By A. S. Whitburn

*From "The Antiquaries Journal," Vol. VII, by permission
of the Society of Antiquaries of London*

still standing in their places) and the temple kitchen. This was a very necessary feature of the temple and occupied quite a large space; there was an open court with a well and fireplaces for heating water and a brick table for the cutting up of the carcasses of the animals; here too the grain was ground on flat saddle-shaped querns of hard stone; off it opened two roofed chambers, one containing the beehive-shaped bread-oven, the other the cooking-range of fire-clay with flat top and circular flues; here were prepared the meals both of the goddess and of her priests and servants.

South-east of the Gig-Par-Ku, the temple of Nin-gal, stood the houses of some of the priests, then more temples—these too ruined now for their character to be certainly known, and then a large and massive building of burnt brick which would appear to be the royal palace whose construction was begun by Ur-Nammu and finished by his son Dungi. One part of it was residential and divided into two sections, perhaps the men's quarters and the harem respectively, for whereas one was easy of access, the other was approached only by roundabout ways through several doors: the major part contained the public rooms where the king gave audience. It has been remarked already that the personnel of the temple duplicated that of the king's court; it was also true that the temple, as the god's house, reproduced the features of the palace of the earthly ruler. The king upon his throne received the obeisance of his subjects, the statue on its base that of the god's worshippers; it was a difference of degree only, and that difference was very small in a country where custom deified the king. Consequently we find that this part of the palace is scarcely to be distinguished from a temple in the arrangement of its outer and inner courts, its antechambers, and its sanctuary-like throne-room; the sacred character of the home of the divine ruler was further emphasized by the fact that it lay within, though on the outskirts of, the Temenos, the great terraced and walled area within which stood the Ziggurat and all the temples described above, the core of the city and its ultimate stronghold.

For all these buildings were linked together to form a single complex known as E-gish-shir-gal, and though each possessed its particular name and function, all were included in the 'temple of Nannar' in the wider sense of the word. The enclosure measured some four hundred yards by two hundred and might be compared to the keep of a medieval castle; round it, corresponding to the bailey, stretched the inner town, its houses closely huddled together inside the great enceinte wall built by Ur-Nammu, and beyond that, along the river-bank and between the canals, lay the suburbs, giving to the city a total length of about four miles and a width of a mile and a half. In the town narrow and irregular streets ran between high blank walls pierced only by doorways; they were unpaved and undrained; there was no wheeled traffic in the town, carriage was by porters or by donkeys, and occasionally against the wall of a house there would be a mounting-block for the convenience of riders and the corners of the buildings were rounded off to give easier passage to the beasts of burden.

In the time of the Third Dynasty of Ur and of the succeeding dynasties of Isin and Larsa the well-to-do citizen was housed remarkably well. The ordinary private house conformed more or less to a recognized type, modified merely by the means of the owner and the exigencies of ground-space; the general idea was that of a quadrangle facing inwards on to a court which served as light-well for all the rooms. The front door opened into a little lobby, sometimes provided with a water-jar and a drain for the washing of the feet of those entering, from which one passed directly into the central court; this was paved with brick and in the middle was a drain, a small opening in the pavement below which was a round pipe, 20 or 30 feet long, made of terra-cotta rings set one above the other; there were holes in the sides of the rings and round

27. RESTORATION OF A PRIVATE HOUSE AT UR

From a drawing by A. S. Whitburn, A.R.I.B.A.

(Cf. Fig. 26)

them there was a packing of broken pottery which
kept the earth from blocking the holes; it was a
seepage drain allowing the water to percolate away
into the subsoil. The house was two stories high
and was built of brick throughout, the lower
courses of burnt brick, the upper of crude brick,
but as the walls seem to have been plastered and
whitewashed all over the difference of material
would not have been noticeable. The ground-floor
rooms had no windows at all—such are indeed
unnecessary in this country of strong suns—but
derived all their light and air through their high
arched doorways; the same was probably true for
the most part of the upper rooms also, but here the
evidence is lacking. A staircase, the lower treads
built of brick, the upper of wood, led from the
court to a wooden gallery running round the inside of the house and giving access to the first-floor
rooms, which were the living-quarters of the
family; the roof made of mud laid over matting
and beams, almost flat but sloping slightly inwards, projected so as to shelter the gallery and
left only a comparatively small opening over the
middle of the court; from its edge gutters stuck
out so as to carry the rain-water into the drain
below.

Of the ground-floor rooms the largest, generally
facing the entrance from the street, was the guest-

chamber or reception-room. The kitchen, with its brick fireplace, was another room, and below the stairs was a lavatory with a drain in its paved floor, while another room was probably for the domestic servants. In some of the houses there was also a private chapel; this was a small chamber, rather narrow, with the pavement at one end slightly raised and on it, against the back wall, a brick altar; either behind the altar or in the side-wall close to it there was a niche or recess intended to receive the cult figure, painting or clay statuette, and close to the altar again a square pillar of brick set against the wall, the meaning of which we do not know. A normal house might therefore contain twelve to fourteen rooms, and though none of these were very large the total accommodation was on a generous scale; of course there were houses smaller than this, and there were others in which a second courtyard with its surrounding chambers might bring the number of rooms to over twenty: in any case the size of the house, its arrangement, and the quality of its construction show that the standard of living was remarkably high and that the public prosperity of the Third Dynasty period was reflected in the comfort of domestic life.

Of the furniture and decoration of the rooms we know little. The interior walls were mud-plastered and whitewashed, the floors spread with matting, but of the actual furniture nothing remains and we must rely upon sculptured representations and notes from inscribed tablets. There were low tables for eating at, often with crossed legs, stools and high-backed chairs with rush seats and cushions, the woodwork of which in wealthy houses might be encased in silver or copper, and beds with wooden frames filled in with string-work or rush; the bedstead might have a tall head-board decorated with figures of birds or flowers. Household vessels were of clay, copper, or stone; baskets and chests made of clay or wood served for storing the clothes of the family. Rugs and carpets adorned the rooms of the better class. At a later period, and perhaps thus early too, there might be affixed to the wall of the room near the door clay reliefs representing gods or demons; these were in the nature of amulets intended to protect the inmates against the spirits of evil and to avert death.

Under the nave of the chapel, if the house boasted such, and if not, under the pavement of any one of the ground-floor rooms, was the burying-place of the family. In most cases this was a brick vault which was opened and reused for each member of the house that died. The dead man, wrapped in matting and wearing his clothes and personal trinkets, was laid in the vault on his side (the bones of the last occupant being unceremoniously bundled away into a corner) with a cup of water held to his lips; the door of the tomb was bricked up, two or three clay vessels containing food were leant against the blocking, the earth put back and the brick pavement relaid over the hole. Sometimes instead of the family vault we find an individual grave, the body laid on the ground at the bottom of the shaft and a bath-shaped clay coffin inverted over it; children are often buried in clay jars or in a bowl over which a second bowl is set upside down as a lid. The custom of burying the dead immediately below the floor of the house seems a strange one, yet it was the general rule. Sometimes, but rarely, occupation ceased after the interment, the front door was walled up and the empty house became a mausoleum; but usually the family continued to live there and the vault was periodically re-used (it is not uncommon to find ten or more bodies in a tomb, and under the floor of one chapel there were thirty infants' graves); it must have been insanitary, and not merely single houses but whole quarters must, one would suppose, in time have become virtually uninhabitable; if this were the case the desertion of a number of houses might help to account for the surprising extent of many ancient Babylonian sites,—the area occupied by the towns is so great and the buildings are so congested that the population seemingly implied exceeds all likelihood; the facts would be more easily understood if we could suppose that at any one time a fair proportion of the houses and even whole districts might be occupied only by the dead.

At the close of the third millennium B.C. burial customs had been modified and the graves of the Third Dynasty contain no such wealth of objects as come from the cemeteries of the fourth millennium to illustrate the art and industries of the early period. Gold ear-rings, sometimes of very delicate granulated work, are almost the only things that represent the goldsmith's craft; the clay and copper vessels are simple and of little interest, though rarely a vase of glazed frit bears witness to a new technique, and the most important documents for art are the cylinder seals. The deep and bold engraving which had made of the seals of the Sargonid age works of the 'grand style' in miniature has by now given place to a cutting more meticulous, very assured, regular and clean, but invention and design have suffered. The subject is monotonously the same and only the details change; the owner of the seal is shown being led by his particular patron deity into the presence of Nannar or some other of the greater gods; but in spite of this limitation many of the seals are extraordinarily fine and the royal seals are veritable gems of engraving. In striking contrast to these are the terra-cottas, the other most interesting objects from the graves, for here the execution is summary —though the moulds may well have been better than the rough impressions struck from them would lead one to suppose—but the subjects are more varied and the treatment is strong and free. The terra-cottas, either figurines in the round taken from a two-piece mould, or reliefs, represent gods and their worshippers; in the case of the latter the range of types is limited, or rather there are a great many repetitions of the same types showing only minor variations and a smaller number of more individual pieces, but the god figures possess the peculiar interest of being in many cases copies, more or less free, of the cult statues in the temples, so that from them we can get some idea of the great works of sculpture. It was inevitable that most of the latter should disappear; if they were of metal they have been melted down, if of stone they have been smashed by iconoclasts and their fragments dispersed; they were not hidden away in graves where they might have been preserved, but exposed in temples to the covetousness or malice of any enemy, and even the rough clay copies of them therefore possess especial value. How fine the originals were is shown by the little salvage that is left; two female heads from

Ur, one in black diorite, one in white marble with eyes inlaid with shell and lapis lazuli, illustrate an art unsuspected before in Mesopotamia. In the short period that had elapsed since the making of the Gudea statues the Sumerian sculptor has advanced not only in technique but in his ideals; here there is the definite striving after beauty which inspired the Greek artist but is seldom found amongst the natives of hither Asia; it requires no effort, no special understanding of an alien mentality to appreciate such works of art as these. The great stela of Ur-Nammu also is very fine but, partly because the subjects are more stereotyped and partly because the medium of bas-relief was more in use and by use more conventionalized, it lacks the spirituality of the heads and if compared with the stela of Gudea betrays but slight signs of progress. It is curious how little material we have for judging the art of the Third Dynasty, considering that this was one of the great periods in Sumerian history and probably one of the most productive, and for the most part there is nothing to indicate that the craftsmen of the time were even on the level of those of a thousand years before; indeed, there would seem to have been a steady process of degeneration implying that the Sumerian genius was played out; only architecture and sculpture in the round, two arts which answer the demands and require the patronage of an imperial and luxurious age, equal or outstrip the efforts of a younger civilization.

From Dungi, at the end of his long and prosperous reign, Bur-Sin inherited the title 'King of Ur, king of the four quarters of the earth' together with the vast empire which justified the boast, and on his accession he was admitted, as his father had been, into the pantheon of the empire's gods. It is noteworthy that he, his son, and his grandson alike have names Semitic in form, and this may well have been a concession to the growing power of the Semitic race. The expansion of the empire westwards had made such concessions more politic, for besides the Akkadians the ruler of Ur had now to reckon with the Amorites of the upper Euphrates and of northern Syria, while to the north the Semitic-speaking land of Assyria had become an important province ruled by a governor appointed from Ur (the name of one Zariqu, the governor, is preserved on a tablet in which he dedicates a temple to 'his Lady Belti-Ekallim, for the life of Bur-Sin the mighty, king of Ur'). The mixed character of the empire is well illustrated by a collection of tablets found in Cappadocia, at Kultepe in the Halys basin: here there was a trading colony whose merchants used Sumerian seals and employed Sumerian scribes, but their language, a dialect of Semitic, connects them not with the south country but with Assyria, and the names of the months and the system of dating by eponym officials is another link with Asshur; the dependence of the outlying parts of the realm on the capital city must have been loose. Sumer had gained its position through moral and cultural supremacy; now that rivals had learned so much the maintenance of power required a force which Sumer by itself could not afford and to secure it the Semites had to be placated and employed.

During the reign of Bur-Sin policy prevailed: the only wars which he had to wage were against the turbulent mountaineers of the Zagros range. Gimil-Sin, who succeeded him after nine years, also had to face troubles eastwards of the Tigris, but the mere record of his campaign fails, perhaps deliberately, to give a full picture of the decay which was already setting in. The *patesi* of Lagash, a city in the heart of Sumer, was made governor of Urbillum (the district of Arbela), of Subartu, Khamasi, Gankhar, Gutebum, and Kardaka. It is obvious that this man, Arad-Nannar, could not from Lagash, where he continued to reside, adequately administer a number of distant provinces east of the Tigris, precisely those which most consistently gave trouble and required firm control on the spot; yet the fact that after the third year of

Gimil-Sin no local governors of those provinces are mentioned proves that Arad-Nannar was not exercising his powers by proxy. We must conclude that he was *patesi in partibus infidelium* and that the provinces in question had shaken off their allegiance to Ur. Susa still kept to its allegiance and its *patesi* could build a temple in honour of the king of Ur, but that he should have a new title, 'Master of the defences', shows that the position was none too secure. Equally symptomatic is an inscription from Umma recording the building by Gimil-Sin of the wall 'Murik-Tidnim', the 'Wall which keeps off the Tidanu' or Amorites of the Anti-Lebanon. Former emperors had preserved their western trade-routes by more offensive action; this building of a wall tells not only of danger in the west but of weakness in dealing with it.

Disaster was not long delayed. Ibi-Sin in the early years of his reign is still mainly concerned with the hill-people of the north-east, and his wars against them and against Susa and Anshan seem to have been successful, though his victories do not appear to have resulted in any recovery of territory, at least there are no mentions of officials appointed to rule the rebellious provinces where the fighting had taken place. That few monuments mentioning his name are extant and that outside Ur itself business documents dated by his reign

all fall within its earlier years may be due to the
accidents of survival and does not necessarily
imply any gradual loss of empire; so far as we
know, when after twenty-five years the end came,
it came suddenly.

An Amorite, Ishbi-Irra of Mari, rose in revolt
and marching down from the middle Euphrates
invaded Akkad; he occupied the city of Isin and
opened negotiations with Elam. Ibi-Sin sent
orders to the governor of the province of Kazallu
to take action against the rebel; probably he hoped
to cut communications between the conspirators
and at the same time to crush his enemy in the
north by a flank attack. But the attempt, whatever it was, was unsuccessful. While Akkad was
in the hands of the Amorites the Elamite forces
crossed the Tigris and overran Sumer; 'Ur was
smitten with weapons' and its unfortunate king
taken captive and carried away to Anshan. The
ruins of Ur bear witness to the savagery with which
the Elamites revenged their long subjection to its
rule; the great buildings of the Third Dynasty
have shared a common fate of wanton destruction,
the sacred vessels of the temples, the treasured
offerings of ancient kings, were looted, and such
as were not worth carrying away were smashed to
pieces; it was now that the stela of Ur-Nammu was
broken up, so that fragments of it were used as

building material in the succeeding age: the imperial city was utterly laid waste.

When they overthrew, when order they destroyed
Then like a deluge all things together (the Elamite) consumed.
Whereunto, Oh Sumer! did they change thee?
The sacred dynasty from the temple they exiled,
They demolished the city, they demolished the temple,
They seized the rulership of the land.
By the command of Enlil order was destroyed,
By the Storm-Spirit of Anu hastening over the land it was seized away.
Enlil directed his eyes towards a strange land.
The divine Ibi-Sin was carried to Elam.

So runs a lamentation of which the text has been found at Nippur, and throughout all later history the name of Ibi-Sin was associated with the omens of disaster.

VI

ISIN AND LARSA

THE poet of Nippur was right when in his lamentation over the downfall of Ibi-Sin he spoke not of Ur alone but of Sumer, for the fate of the city involved that of the whole land and people. From the destruction wrought by the Amorites and the Elamites the Sumerians never recovered and their history as an independent nation stops at this point. For a long time the process of decay had been going on; by intermixture with Akkadians and other Semitic-speaking stocks the purity of the race had been lost and the numbers of those who could call themselves Sumerians had diminished until they formed a minority only of the population; parallel with this physical decay there had been a moral degeneration which is reflected in the art of the people, where softness has taken the place of strength and convention has swamped originality. When the political predominance which had been precariously won and upheld by collaboration with the Akkadian element was now violently wrested from them they had not energy to recover it. On the other hand, old traditions of independence and hegemony died hard, and abortive attempts were made by different cities and at various times to revive the glories of the past: the only result was to plunge the country into a welter of civil war and to usher in once more an era of division into city-states; Isin, Larsa, Erech, Sippar, Babylon, and Kish were to have kings of their own, and in their squabbles the man-power and the morale of the south country was frittered away.

Ishbi-Irra established himself at Isin and founded a dynasty which lasted for five generations and enjoyed fairly wide dominion; from the outset he obtained control of Ur, whose ruins his successors took it in hand to rebuild, Erech, and part at least of the north country; possibly the rule of Isin stretched on occasions as far as Nineveh. But at the same time an independent state arose at Larsa, only seventy miles from Isin at the head of the marshes which extended along the east bank of the lower Euphrates to the head of the Persian Gulf. That this should have been possible is curious and difficult to explain in view of the un-doubted power of the Isin kings who were scarcely likely to be patient of a rival so close to their doors. It has been suggested that the explanation lies in the inaccessible character of the marshes which in later history formed the domain of the 'kings of the Sea Lands' and seldom acknowledged the control even of the great rulers of Babylon; their scattered inhabitants might easily defy a power which could overawe the cities of the west bank, exposed to the attack of land troops, and the natural political base for them would be on the marsh's edge, to the north, where they could link up with the trade-routes of the river valley. There is much in this view to commend it, but even so the difficulty remains that though the marshlands were safe from invasion the city of Larsa, the core of their resistance, was open to assault and the terrain favoured the attacking forces rather than the marshmen, who would find it not easy to reinforce the defence; yet Isin does not seem to have attempted a blow at the rival capital, on the contrary the relations between the two cities remained friendly throughout the reign of Ishbi-Irra's dynasty. The influence of Elam may account for this. For the overthrow of the Third Dynasty of Ur the king of Anshan and Ishbi-Irra of Mari had made common cause and the former had apparently borne the brunt of the campaign in the south; he would naturally expect his share in the spoils of war, territorially as well as in the form of loot, yet there is no sign of any direct Elamite control permanently influenced over Sumer; it would not be rash to conclude that control was exercised indirectly and that Naplanum, who founded the Larsa dynasty, was a nominee and vassal of the

Elamite king. As such, supported by the redoubt-
able armies of Anshan, Larsa might well be
immune from attack by Isin even after the bond
of alliance between Anshan and Ishbi-Irra had
worn thin; hostilities between the two cities only
begin at a time when Larsa was in revolt against
Elam and had to rely on its own strength.

So frankly acknowledged was the prestige of
Sumer that the conqueror from Mari at once
transferred his capital from the middle Euphrates
to Isin; and so impregnated was even the Amorite
north with Sumerian culture that his immediate
task was the rehabilitation of the Sumerian towns
laid waste by the invaders. At Ur the names
of Gimil-ilishu, Ishme-Dagan and Lipit-Ishtar
appear constantly on the bricks of temples once
destroyed by Elam. Gimil-ilishu brought back to
Ur the statue of Nannar which the Elamite conquerors had carried off to Anshan. Ishme-Dagan
revived old memories by adopting the title 'King
of Sumer and Akkad', and Enannatum, the son of
Lipit-Ishtar, was made high priest of Nannar
and during his term of office rebuilt the great
temple of Nin-gal which Bur-Sin had founded.
An optimist might have thought that a Sumerian
renaissance was still within the bounds of possibility although the ruling power had been usurped
by Semites.

For one moment such hopes seemed to be justified, for Lipit-Ishtar came to a violent end (the details are unknown) and was succeeded on the throne by one Ur-Ninurta who, whatever his origin, is shown by his name to have been of Sumerian stock. He claimed dominion over 'the four quarters of the earth' and did in fact control the western delta from Nippur to the sea: his rise to power involved almost immediate hostilities with Larsa. Gungunum of Larsa had been on excellent terms with Isin, so much so that when Enannatum built his temple he made of it an offering for the life of Gungunum, implying for Libit-Ishtar a friendship little short of vassalage, and Larsa was not likely to welcome the advent of a Sumerian adventurer to the Isin throne. Gungunum was at the time engaged with a war, perhaps a revolt, against Elam, but as soon as that was brought to a successful conclusion he set his house in order against his new enemy and built forts and a city wall as a preliminary to war. The first clash of arms was in favour of Ur-Enurta and Gungunum was apparently killed on the field, but his son Abi-sare carried on the struggle and seemingly with more success; no records dealing with the vicissitudes of the war survive, but at Ur, a stronghold of the Isin kings and one of their main possessions in Sumer, the names of Ur-Enurta and his successors fail

altogether whereas Abi-sare, Sumu-ilum and the
following kings of Larsa all have monuments to
their credit; it can only mean that the city had
passed from the hands of Isin to those of Larsa as
early as the time of Abi-sare if not in the days of
Gungunum and Lipit-Ishtar, and that the title
assumed by Ur-Enurta, 'benefactor of Ur and
Eridu', was in the nature of an empty boast. The
attempted 'Sumerian revival' had not seriously
affected Ur except that it brought a change of
masters; before long another change came. The
independence won or maintained by Gungunum
through his war with Anshan was ill tolerated by
Elam, and Sumu-ilum by his campaigns directed
against Kazallu must have further embittered
relations without adding to his territory. A new
power had arisen in the north, where Western
Semitic immigrants had established an independent dynasty in Babylon and by intrigue or conquest were making themselves a real danger to
the southern monarchies; a fresh revolution had
brought to an end the Sumerian dynasty of Isin
without improving the relations between that city
and Larsa; Nur-Adad was able to keep the peace
for the space of sixteen years, but Sin-iddinam was
faced with a war against Elam, now in alliance with
Isin, and after two more short reigns by kings of his
house we find an Elamite on the throne of Larsa.

The details of the campaign are not known, but Kudur-Mabug of Elam, probably in alliance with Isin and Babylon, invaded Larsa, crushed Silli-Adad, who had only reigned for one year, and organized it as a vassal state under the rule of his son Warad-Sin; with Larsa went Ur, Eridu, Lagash, and Nippur; Erech was a separate kingdom also perhaps subject to Elam. For all practical purposes the delta was now divided into three states, Larsa, Isin, and Babylon, with the growing power of Assyria to the north; of these Isin and Babylon would naturally tend to gravitate together, Isin and Larsa were bound first to come to blows and there could be little doubt that Larsa was the stronger of the two. Rim-Sin who succeeded Warad-Sin, after many campaigns in which he had sometimes to meet Babylonian forces allied with his immediate enemy, in the thirtieth year of his reign captured and laid waste the city of Isin and set the stage for the final struggle between the Babylonian Semites and the South.

It was the obvious policy for the Larsa kings, foreigners as they were, to placate Sumerian feeling in order to win support against Babylon. Kudur-Mabug began by strengthening the defences of the city of Ur: although his political capital was at Larsa, the old imperial city came in for much attention on his part, and for control of the south it was essential; moreover, Ur gave him the command of the head of the Persian Gulf, with which Ur-Nammu's canal afforded direct communication for ships, and therefore of the sea-borne trade, still a factor of tremendous importance. The Ziggurat with its walled terrace has been described as the ultimate stronghold of the city; an earlier king of Larsa had strengthened with a revetment of burnt brick the original mud-brick wall of the terrace; Kudur-Mabug added to this a corner fort with tower and sally-port, and both he and his successor Rim-Sin were lavish in building new temples and in restoring old; their buildings have for the most part perished, but their inscribed foundation-cones bear witness to their pious zeal. In this too the Elamite conquerors were following the example set by the native kings of Larsa; Nur-Adad had rebuilt E-Nun-Makh, the temple of Nannar and Nin-gal; both he and his son Sin-idinnam restored the ziggurat of Eridu, the ancient centre of the worship of Ea, and at Ur Sin-idinnam and all three of the succeeding kings of his line, including even the short-lived Silli-Adad, left their record in temple-construction. Sumerian religion had been so readily adopted by the Semitic subjects of the old empire that the possession of its ancient sacred places was a valu-able asset and the pious care of its temples was a

bid for the support not only of Sumerian national-
ists but of a far wider circle of believers. The
religious weapon was particularly effective as
against Babylon at this period, for the western
Semites installed there were pushing the claims
of the local Semitic god Marduk, who had hitherto
commanded slight allegiance outside his own
boundaries, but must now needs assume a pre-
eminence proportionate to the political influence
of his city; against this upstart the south could
muster the forces of tradition, and Akkadians as
well as Sumerians might be expected to answer
to the appeal.

This is probably the reason why in the decadence
of the Sumerian nation we find the period of their
greatest literary and historical activity. It was
under the Larsa Dynasty that the scribes took in
hand the composition of those historical works of
which the King-lists are a digest and the late
Babylonian Chronicle an echo. They collected
the books of Omens and not only explained the
meaning of the signs in the liver of the sacrificial
victim or of natural phenomena but illustrated
them by precedents drawn from history; they
redacted the temple hymns; they set down in
writing the old legends which told of the cosmo-
gony, the Deluge, the deeds of the demi-gods, and
they drew up the list of the official pantheon. It

is a strange fact that the great days of the Third Dynasty of Ur have left us virtually no trace of any literary records of this sort; the antiquarian zeal of the scribes was only kindled in the decadence, but these by their studious labours set the seal to the conquest which their forefathers had made with the sword. The Semitic-speaking peoples of Mesopotamia, Akkadians, Amorites, Assyrians, had accepted Sumerian religion together with Sumerian culture; that religion was now reduced to a system, and that system inspired by intense Sumerian patriotism and intolerance of anything foreign, and so complete was the moral subordination of the Semites that even this almost defiant manifesto of a conquered and dying race acquired pontifical authority. Not a single Semitic god found his way into the official pantheon or was mentioned in the liturgies, even though he might still have a place in popular worship. The forms of service as well as the stories concerning the gods were fixed according to purely Sumerian traditions; but the Semites translated into their own tongue the canon from which everything Semitic had been so sedulously excluded, and two thousand years later the Assyrians of Nineveh were still bound by the legacy of a people whose very name they had forgotten.

But for this the historian of the Sumerians might

have concluded his task with the lamentation over the downfall of Ibi-Sin: as it is, the long-drawn death-agony of the race is of importance because it gave them time to assure their immortality. No sooner was the work done than final disaster overtook Sumer. Under the kings of Larsa they had enjoyed favour though deprived of independence; Rim-Sin, after his conquest of Isin which made him master of the whole south country, was necessarily the champion of Sumer as against the western Semites of the First Dynasty of Babylon, and if he was known to his enemies as 'king of Ur' it may be that he hoped, by reviving memories of Ur-Nammu, Dungi, and Bur-Sin, to pose as something more than an alien ruler. But the long period of internecine warfare had weakened and impoverished the south, and in the meanwhile there had arisen in Babylon a leader of very different calibre from the kings his predecessors. Hammurabi came to the throne immediately after Rim-Sin's victory over Isin, an ally which the Babylonian forces under his father had failed to protect: Babylon had suffered materially and in prestige, and the new king's first concern was to restore order at home; six years later he wrested Isin and Erech from the hands of Larsa, nullifying the results of Rim-Sin's victory and re-establishing the credit of his own city. For twenty-five years he rested on his laurels, then, when Rim-Sin was a very old man (he had been on the throne for sixty-one years), he launched a fresh attack on him, defeated the armies of Elam, captured Larsa, and made himself undisputed master of Sumer. In the temple of Nin-gal at Ur the king of Babylon set up a diorite stela recording his exploits; there is no mention of any assault upon the city, in the ruins no evidence of destruction; the fortune of war had exchanged one foreign ruler for another, and Ur had accepted the change apparently with indifference.

There was to be one more flicker of independence, though whether this was due to Sumerian feeling as such cannot be said. A quarter of a century later, in the eleventh year of Samsu-iluna, Hammurabi's son, the south rose in revolt. Within a twelvemonth it was crushed. The twelfth year of Samsu-iluna was described as that in which 'he razed the walls of Ur'; excavation has shown that in this very year the temples of Ur were plundered and burnt and whole quarters of the town devastated; Babylon punished rebellion with a heavy hand. Other cities of Sumer shared the same fate, and so far as history goes that was the end. Of the Sumerians nothing more is heard. Their language, though fallen out of popular use, might long survive in religious texts to be studied by the curious and painfully understood by the aid of a dictionary; but the race had gone, exhausted by wars, sapped by decay, swamped by the more vigorous stock which had eaten of the tree of their knowledge.

VII

THE CLAIM OF SUMER

THREE generations ago the existence of the Sumerians was unknown to the scientific world; to-day their history can be written and their art illustrated more fully than that of many ancient peoples. It is the history and the art of a race which died out nearly four thousand years ago, whose very name had been forgotten before the beginning of our era, and it might well be asked whether the knowledge recently acquired is not merely a matter of curiosity, whether the Sumerians at all deserve this literary resurrection. It is true that a novel discovery is liable to upset our perspective and an individual or a nation may from an accident of discovery or from the intrinsic excellence of their products assume an importance altogether out of proportion to the rôle they have filled in history: the records of man's activities, the works of his hands, are never without interest, but those activities may end in a blind alley, the works be isolated examples of art doing no more than illustrate how the human mind reacts to certain stimuli; the real criterion of value is, how far have these people contributed to human progress? what part had they in forming that culture

which is the heritage of the living world? and it is
by this standard that we must estimate the importance of the civilization now rescued from
oblivion.

The earliest cemetery found at Ur, with its
royal graves and wonderfully rich furniture, has
been assigned to a date of, in round figures, 3500
B.C. The date is admittedly vague, based on the
lowest estimate for that of the First Dynasty of
Ur, 3100 B.C., and allowing for a reasonable lapse
of time during which the existence of these royal
graves, sanctified as they were by the wholesale
slaughter of human victims and by the deification
of their occupants, could be forgotten and their site
violated by the intrusion of fresh interments. To
this theoretical argument has to be added that
of succession in the graves themselves and the
development of fashions in their structure and
contents, and even if it be supposed that the graves
form a continuous series coming down to the
beginning of the First Dynasty, the earliest of them
must none the less be more ancient by wellnigh
four hundred years.

Now this means that the earliest graves of Ur
are somewhat older than the First Dynasty of
Egypt. Egyptian chronology has been a subject
of much dispute and very different conclusions
have been reached for the date of the unification

of the two prehistoric kingdoms under Menes; the most conservative view, which also is that held by the majority of scholars, would put this about 3300 B.C.; but whether this be accepted or not, the fact remains that the chronologies of Egypt and of Mesopotamia are so far interdependent that if Menes be placed further back in time the same thing must be done for Sumerian history and the relation between the two countries must be left unaltered: here the shorter chronology is adopted for both countries, but the positive date is for the purposes of the argument of little importance and the essential point is the relation between the two whereby the graves of Ur are as old as or older than Menes.

Three things have to be compared: the contents of the Ur graves, the contents of the royal graves of the First Egyptian Dynasty discovered by Professor Flinders Petrie at Abydos, and the character of the predynastic civilization of the Nile Valley. The prehistoric civilization of Egypt and that of Sumer have nothing in common. Between the prehistoric art of Egypt and that of its First Dynasty there is a very great difference, not so complete as to amount to a breach of continuity but enough to mark an epoch; the changes are coming in towards the end of the predynastic period and by the time of 'Menes' we have what is virtually a new culture.

It has long been recognized that this rapid development, which laid the foundations of what we know as Egyptian civilization, was due to some foreign influence, and it has long been remarked that the developed civilization presents in its early stages certain features common to the Euphrates valley, for instance, cylinder seals, pear-shaped mace-heads of stone, a panelled construction in building, features which appear suddenly with no apparent antecedents and subsequently disappear altogether, whereas in Mesopotamia they would seem to be native and persist in history. To these common features we can now add more, the use of the sistrum, a musical instrument too peculiar to have originated independently in two places, certain types of stone vases, grotesque animal drawings, and over and above such material resemblances there are elements in the religion of Egypt which would seem to be derived from Sumerian mythology. Even if the character of the borrowings left any doubt as to which country was indebted to the other, which indeed they do not, the argument of priority in date would be decisive. The Egyptians traced back the beginnings of their history to Menes, before whom came darkness and the demi-gods, and the discoveries of archaeology have justified their belief; for the Sumerians the First Dynasty of Ur came at the

end of a period of civilization whose duration was
to be reckoned in thousands of years, and though
recent excavations have carried us back but a
little way into that legendary period, yet they do
substantiate in principle the Sumerian contention.
Nobody looking at the contents of the graves,
themselves older than Menes, can fail to see that
they belong to a civilization already old if not
actually decadent. Nothing is in an experimental
stage; on the contrary, art is subject to conventions
so stereotyped that it is hard to distinguish between objects which are demonstrably hundreds
of years apart in age, there is a technique, especially in metallurgy, which could only result
from centuries of apprenticeship—the Egyptians
never in their best periods produced weapons as
good as the socketed axes and adzes of early
Sumer,—and the potter's wheel, introduced into
Egypt well on in the Old Kingdom, had been used
by the Sumerians for long ages. In the time of
'Menes' not only was the cultural level of Mesopotamia far higher than that of Egypt, but whereas
the civilization of Egypt was a novelty, that of
Sumer was ancient; Sumerian civilization, whatever its ultimate origin, had developed in its own
country and on its own lines for so long that it
could fairly by now be called endemic, while that
of Egypt was inspired and made possible by the

introduction of foreign models and foreign blood. The character of the borrowings and the proximity of the superior culture leave no alternative source for the influence which affected Egypt at the close of its predynastic age; directly or indirectly that came from southern Mesopotamia.

In the course of this history emphasis has been laid upon the fact that Sumerian arms and Sumerian commerce not only spread up the valleys of the Tigris and Euphrates but obtained a firm foothold in Syria and penetrated into Asia beyond the Taurus, so that from the very outset there was imposed upon these more backward countries at least a veneer of Sumerian civilization. Had that civilization died with the race which originated it the early conquests might have had but an ephemeral effect, but such was not the case. In Mesopotamia the political extinction of the Sumerians made astonishingly little difference to culture. The old laws of Sumer became with very slight modifications the code of Babylon: religion was unaffected, and though the gods preferred to be called by Semitic names, they were the old Sumerian gods and no Semitic deity could obtain official recognition: the Sumerian language fell into disuse, but its literature was translated for the benefit of the Semitic reader: the arts maintained their old traditions so well that even the wall-sculptures of eighth-century Assyria, individual as they appear, betray their parentage with works of the Third Dynasty of Ur and of the fourth millennium B.C. The whole civilization of Babylon, and in a scarcely less degree that of Assyria, are rooted in the alien past, as their own historians of the decadence confessed.

Berossus, writing in the fourth or third century before Christ, describes a race of monsters half man and half fish which, led by one Oannes, came out of the Persian Gulf and settling in the coast towns of Sumer introduced the arts of writing, agriculture, and working in metal; 'in a word,' he declares, 'all the things that make for the amelioration of life were bequeathed to men by Oannes, and since that time no further inventions have been made.'

Sumerian genius evolved a civilization which persisted for nearly fifteen hundred years after its authors had vanished, and Babylon and Nineveh did not keep this heritage to themselves; they also were imperial peoples, and their dominion over or their intercourse with the west fostered in those lands the seed which earlier Sumerian conquerors had planted. The Hittites of Asia Minor adopted the cuneiform script which was one of the greatest of the Sumerian inventions; Babylonian became the diplomatic language of the courts of Syria and

even of Egypt; the cylinder seals of Syria and
Cappadocia are both in form and in style derived
from Mesopotamia; the sculptures of Carchemish
trace their descent through Assyria to Sumer; the
eclectic art of the Phoenicians in so far as it drew
from Oriental models was in the same indirect
way an offshoot of the Sumerian. This is not to
say that these countries were slavish copyists of a
civilization which had as a matter of fact passed
clean out of their ken; in each of them the arts
developed in a normal way and received a more
or less distinctive stamp of their nationality. But
on each of them the Sumerian tradition has had
a profound influence, stronger, naturally, in the
home lands of the lower river valleys where it is
indeed the direct begetter of all that is to follow,
more subtle in the outlying provinces where it is a
collateral rather than a source; and through these
later peoples of the Near East it has influenced the
material civilization of the modern world.

Such a claim is not easy to establish by concrete
example, partly because we can seldom, if ever,
know all the links in so long a chain, partly because the arts are not static and the inspiration
which originates also modifies and transmutes so
that its first and its final manifestation may seem
to have nothing at all in common. But an instance
of plain indebtedness may illustrate a wider truth.

The arch in building was unknown in Europe
until the conquests of Alexander, when Greek
architects fastened eagerly on this, to them, novel
feature and they, and later the Romans, introduced to the western world what was to be the
distinguishing element in architecture. Now the
arch was a commonplace of Babylonian construction—Nebuchadnezzar employed it freely in the
Babylon which he rebuilt in 600 B.C.; at Ur there
is still standing an arch in a temple of Kuri-Galzu,
king of Babylon about 1400 B.C.; in private houses
of the Sumerian citizens of Ur in 2000 B.C. the
doorways were arched with bricks set in true
voussoir fashion; an arched drain at Nippur must
date to about 3000 B.C.; true arches roofing the
royal tombs at Ur now carry back the knowledge
of the principle another four or five hundred years.
Here is a clear line of descent to the modern world
from the dawn of Sumerian history. What is true
of the arch is true also of the dome and the vault.
Here, where the principle once invented is fixed
for all time and only minor changes in form can be
introduced, the sequence is easier to follow than in
the more fluid arts of design: the influence of
Sumer on the plastic art of later peoples is perhaps
just as real, but it can be apprehended rather
than demonstrated. But it is in the more abstract
realm of ideas that the Sumerians have most

obviously and most directly contributed to the development of western civilization, through the Hebrew people. Not only did the Semites adopt ready-made those stories of the Creation and the Flood which viewed as history or as parable have affected the Christian even more than the Jewish Church; the Jewish religion, as it owed not a little of its origin to the Sumerian, so also was throughout the period of the Kings and the Captivity brought into close contact with the Babylonian worship which was taken over from Sumer, and partly by its precept and partly in opposition to it attained to higher growth. The laws of Moses were largely based on Sumerian codes, those same codes which lay at the bottom of the great Code of Hammurabi, and so from the Sumerians the Hebrews derived the ideals of social life and justice which informed all their history and have by Christian races been regarded in theory if not in practice as criteria for their own customs and enactments. The difficulty lies not in recognizing the fact but in estimating the importance of the debt which the modern world owes to this race so recently rescued from complete oblivion. If human effort is to be judged merely by its attainment, then the Sumerians, with due allowance made for date and circumstance, must be accorded a very honourable though not a pre-eminent place;

28. TWO STATUE-HEADS OF THE PERIOD OF THE THIRD DYNASTY OF UR

One in black diorite, the other in white marble with eyes inlaid with lapis lazuli and shell

if by its effect on human history, they merit higher rank. Their civilization, lighting up a world still plunged in primitive barbarism, was in the nature of a first cause. We have outgrown the phase when all the arts were traced to Greece and Greece was thought to have sprung, like Pallas, full-grown from the brain of the Olympian Zeus; we have learnt how that flower of genius drew its sap from Lydians and Hittites, from Phoenicia and Crete, from Babylon and Egypt. But the roots go farther back: behind all these lies Sumer. The military conquests of the Sumerians, the arts and crafts which they raised to so high a level, their social organization and their conceptions of morality, even of religion, are not an isolated phenomenon, an archaeological curiosity; it is as part of our own substance that they claim our study, and in so far as they win our admiration we praise our spiritual forebears.

29. Shell plaque from the grave of
Queen Shub-ad

British Museum

INDEX

A-anni-padda, 33, 40, 41, 44.
Abi-sare, 174, 175.
Abraham, 103, 117.
Abydos, 185.
Adab, 83, 84, 132, 137.
Adapa, 122.
Adonis, 30, 122.
Agade, dynasty of, 62 seq.;
  downfall of, 83.
Akshak, 66.
Amara, 76.
Amelu, 95 ff.
Amurru, 4, (165), (167).
Anshan, 62, 81, 86, 136, 167,
  172, 173, 175.
Anu, 128, 169.
Apsu, 150.
Arad-Nannar, 166.
Arbil, 74, 166.
Arch, use of, 37, 147, 158, 191.
Architecture, 37, 142.
Art, prehistoric, 42 ff., 78;
  under Gudea, 86; under
  Third Dynasty, 162 ff.; in-
  fluences, 186–9.
Ashur-natsir-pal, 135.
Asshur, 27, 47, 74; (Assyria),
  165, 176.
Astarabad treasure, 47.
Awan, 64.

Babbar, 71.
'Babel', tower of, 142.
Babylon, 45, 119, 122, 137,
  142, 171, 189, 191; rise of
  First Dynasty at, 175, 180.
Baghdad, 1, 74.
Berossus, 27, 189.

Bur-Sin of Isin, 174.
Bur-Sin of Ur, 131, 139, 146,
  147, 165.
Bur-Sin, shrine of, at Ur, 151.

Canals, 17, 66, 68, 113, 132.
Cappadocia, 46, 49, 79, 82,
  116, 165, 189.
Carchemish, painted pottery at,
  10; trade route, 115; sculp-
  ture, 189.
Caucasus, 46.
Chronology, errors in, 29, 62.
Cilicia, 46.
Codes of law, 69, 90, 91, 192
  (*see under* Hammurabi).
Costume, changes in, 77–8.
Cyprus, 79.

Deification of kings, 30, 68, 83,
  128, 130, 165.
Delta, development of, 2–3.
Der, 74.
Diabekr, 76, 82.
dikud, 93.
Dilmun, 116.
Drehem, sacred farm at, 140.
Dublal-makh, 147.
Dubrum, 89.
Dumuzi, 30.
Dungi, 54, 60, 91, 130, 136 ff.,
  154.

Ea (Enki), 121, 122, 137, 177.
Eannatum, 38, 50, 55, 57, 63,
  66, 67.
E-gish-shir-gal, 155.
Egypt, cultural connexions
  with, 46, 184 f.

Flam, 46, 58, 64, 67, 79, 80, 82, 86, 168, 171, 175; Elamite dynasty at Larsa, 175 f.; defeat of, 181.
Elamite civilization, 7, 9.
Enannatum the priest, 151, 173.
Enannatum of Lagash, 68.
Enlil, 119, 121, 128, 139, 140, 169.
Entemena, 67, 68, 86.
Entu, 106.
E-nun-makh, 145, 177.
Erech, 29, 30, 33, 35, 41, 48, 64, 67, 70, 71, 73, 82, 84, 91, 107, 119, 130, 137, 171.
Eridu, 8, 10, 121, 132, 137, 176, 177.
E-sagila, 137.
Etana, 30, 122.
E-temen-ni-il, 144.

Fara, 27.
Flood, 28, 30, 31 ff., 48, 122 ff., 192.

Ga-makh, 145.
Ganes, 49, 79, 116.
Gankhar, 166.
Ga-nun-makh, 121.
Gig-par-ku, 154.
Gilgamesh, 30, 31, 122.
Gimil-ilishu, 173.
Gimil-Sin, 166, 167.
Gudea, 85 ff., 111, 128, 130.
Gulf, Persian, original extent of, 1; trade in, 46, 116.
Gungunum, 174, 175.
Gutebum, 166.
Guti, 5, 74, 83; invasion by, 83, 84, 85; downfall of, 88, 89.

Hagar, 103.
Hammâm, 47.
Hammurabi, 45, 180, 181; code of, 50, 58, 91 seq., 111, 192.
Hit, 2, 45, 64.
Hittites, 47, 189.
Human sacrifice, 30, 39, 126.

Ibi-Sin, 167–9, 170, 180.
Ilku tax, 60.
Im-dugud relief, 41.
Indus valley, connexions with Sumer, 8, 46.
Inlay work, 41, 50.
Interest on loans, &c., 118.
Ipkhur-Kish, 82.
Ishakku, 93.
Ishbi-Irra, 168, 171, 172.
Ishme-dagan, 173.
Ishtar, 107, 108, 119, 121.
Isin, 58, 91, 171 ff.; dynasty of, 173, 180.

Jacob, 129.

Kadishtu, 107.
Kardaka, 166.
Karun, 2.
Kazallu, 57, 136, 175.
Khabur, 2, 46.
Khamasi, 64, 166.
Kimash, 136.
King-lists, 21 seq., 28, 41, 62, 177.
Kirkuk, 74.
Kish, 10, 12, 27, 29, 30, 33, 47, 48, 50, 55, 64, 65, 68, 72, 82, 84, 130, 171; palace of, 33, 38.

Ku-Bau, 65.
Kudur-Mabug, 121, 176, 177.
Kultepe, 165.
Kuri-galzu, 191.
Kurna, 1.

Lagash, 58, 63, 66 ff., 76, 85 ff.,
  130, 133, 134, 137, 138, 166,
  176.
Larsa, 119, 132, 171 ff.;
  dynasty of, 175; fall of, 181.
Lebanon, 79, 82, 116.
Lipit-ishtar, 173, 175.
Lugal-banda, 30.
Lugal-ushumgal, 83.
Lugal-zaggisi, 64, 65, 71, 73,
  74, 76, 128.
Lulubu, 82, 136.

Macpelah, 117.
Maer, 137.
Magan, 46, 82, 132.
Malgium, 74.
Manishtusu, 79, 81.
Marduk, 16, 119, 122, 125,
  177.
Mari, 64, 67, 76, 168, 172.
Martu, 4, 5, 12.
mashkim, 93.
Menes, 185.
Mes-anni-padda, 33, 41, 45,
  46, 48, 64.
Mesilim, 65.
Mes-kalam-dug, 38, 43, 53, 54,
  56.
Mes-ki-ag-ga-sir, 30.
Metallurgy, 42.
Money, 117.
Moses, 192.
Mosul, 115.
Muhammerah, 2.

Mushkinu, 95 ff.
Musyan, 9.

Nabonidus, 76.
Nabu, 121.
Nannar, 71, 119, 121, 130, 132,
  135; temple of, at Ur, 81,
  144; high priestesses of, 77,
  83, 107, 139.
Naplanum, 172.
Naram-Sin, 50, 54, 56, 76, 78,
  81, 83.
Nebuchadnezzar, 191.
Nergal, 121.
Nidaba, 71.
Nina, 125.
Nin-e-gal, 132.
Nineveh, 171, 179, 189.
Ningal, 130, 132, 135.
Nin-gal, temple of, at Ur, 150,
  173, 181.
Nin-girsu, 68, 70, 85.
Nin-khursag, 40, 71, 121.
Nippur, 27, 67, 70, 71, 76, 81,
  83, 84, 91, 119, 130, 132,
  137, 138, 139, 140, 169, 176,
  191.
Nisaba and Hani, laws of, 91,
  104.
Noah, 32, 123.
Nur-adad, 175, 177.

Oannes, 189.
Oman, 45.
Opis, 4, 64, 67.

Painted pottery, 9, 10.
Palace, likeness of to temple,
  155.
Pamirs, 46.
Patesi, 18, 66, 83, 85, 93, 128,
  138, 139, 166.

Rachel, 129.
Reed huts, 16, 123.
Rim-Sin, 58, 176, 177, 180.
Rimush, 56, 81.

Sajur, 2.
Sal-Me, 107, 146.
Samsu-iluna, 181.
Sarah, 103.
Sargon of Akkad, 49, 57, 58, 65, 72, 73, 74, 79, 86, 111, 137.
Seripul, 82.
Shamash, 119.
Shargalisharri, 83, 84.
Shatt-al-Arab, 2.
Shatt-al-Hai, 68.
Shinar, 7.
Shub-ad, 40, 43, 54.
Shushinak, 136, 137.
Silli-adad, 176, 177.
Simran, 46.
Sin : *see* Nannar.
Sin-iddinam, 175, 177.
Sippar, 4, 82, 83, 91, 171.
Stela of Ur-Nammu, 134, 168.
Stela of the Vultures, 38, 50, 55, 67.
Subartu, 45, 166.
Sumu-ilum, 116, 175.
Suruppak, 32, 122.
Susa, 9, 81, 91, 136, 137, 167.
Syria, 46, 79, 82, 115, 116, 165, 188, 189.

Tammuz, 30.
Tello, 27, 65, 66, 70, 87, 88.
teraphim, 129.
Tirigan, 89.
Trade, extent at, 45, 49, 79, 85, 86, 115, 116, 165.

al 'Ubaid, 27, 33, 45 ; primitive settlement, 12, 13 ; temple of, 40.
Umma, 57, 67 f., 70, 76, 132, 167.
Ur-Enurta, 174, 175.
Ur-Nammu, 60, 121, 130 ff., 136, 140, 154, 177.
Ur-Nina, 66.
Ur-Ningirsu, 128.
Ur-Ninurta, 174.
Uru-Kagina, 69, 71, 91.
Uta-napishtim, 31, 122.
Ur: royal graves at, 30, 35, 184; First Dynasty of : *see under* Mes-anni-padda and A-anni-padda; fall of, 64; captured by Lagash, 67; captured by Agade, 76, 81; royal priestesses at, 77, 83, 107; Third Dynasty established, 130; buildings of, 140 seq.; fall of Third Dynasty, 168; rebuilt by Kings of Isin and Larsa, 173; subject to Larsa, 176; captured by Babylon, 181.
Ur-Bau, 85.
Utu-Khegal, 89, 190, 130.

Wadi el Batin, 2.
Warad-Sin, 176.
Warka, 27.
Weapons, 53–5.
Wheel, potter's, 187.
Wheeled vehicles, 30, 54.

Zagros, 5, 74, 82, 166.
Ziggurat of Ur, 132, 135, 141 ff., 177.
Zikru, 107.